# RAGE

# RAGE

## MICHAEL EIGEN

WESLEYAN UNIVERSITY PRESS

MIDDLETOWN, CONNECTICUT

Published by Wesleyan University Press,
Middletown, CT 06459

Designed by Richard Hendel
Set in Monotype Garamond and Marie Luise types
by B. Williams & Associates
Manufactured in the United States of America

ISBN 0-8195-6585-7 (cloth)
ISBN 0-8195-6586-5 (pbk.)

Library of Congress Cataloging-in-Publication Data
appear at the back of this book.

5   4   3   2   1

# CONTENTS

A serpent, in the course of its wanderings, came into an armorer's shop. As it glided over the floor, it felt its skin pricked by a file lying there. In a rage, it turned around and tried to dart its fangs into the file, but could do no harm to heavy iron and had to move beyond its rage.

—Aesop fable
And next time?

———

"What is the excess in your nature?" he is asked by Clement.

"I don't know," Cellini replies. "I've had this rage since I was born. It creates and destroys with the same hand."

—John Patrick Shanley, *Cellini*

———

Bataille speaks of "a moment of rage" as the kindling spark of all great works: it cannot be summoned by an act of will, and its source is always extra-literary.

—Paul Auster, *The Art of Hunger*

———

I am seething with rage. A constant force. It is there. It is there. I live my life with all my might, of course, love my kids, bicker with my wife, open worlds with patients, see God in prayer, perhaps beyond God in meditation. But—there is the rage, the rage. They cannot take that away. They will not. The rage of the human.

—Michael Eigen, e-mail to Marilyn Charles

———————

"I'm right, you're wrong," says Rage.

"No, *I'm* right, *you're* wrong," says Rage.

"We're right, we're wrong," says the Yearning for Something More.

"Now what?" asks Something Else.

Rage is trauma.

Rage is traumatizing.

Rage is fusion.

Rage tears fusion.

Rage tries to undo separation.

Rage is separation.

Rage is not-fusion, not-separation.

Rage affirms.

Rage obliterates.

Rage moves from self to self in terror, freezing, fiery fury.

# RAGE

age is aimed at children, lovers, parents, authorities, subordinates, strangers, and ideological, religious, and political causes. If you study rage in your life, you will make your own list.

"Road rage" is a popular term now. It has ancient roots. Oedipus kills his father in a case of road rage. His outburst is a link in a long, complicated chains of events, including roots in childhood abuse and branches, two plays later, in grisly wonder at the forces at work in life.

Infanticide-matricide-patricide. Ancient Greeks puzzled over these urges and explored their permutations in myth and drama. Art not only reflects but also binds and transforms. It masticates events and tendencies that alarm and excite us. One of its functions is antenna-like, to catch new spirits in the air, even create new spirits. But it also tries to work over what it shows, initiating processes of digestion, an emotional, aesthetic digestive process taking thousands of years, perhaps never ending, ever beginning.

Psychotherapy shares many themes with art. It turns configurations of feelings around, chewing on them from multiple viewpoints and in varying ways. One holds on to one's seat, as one becomes party to and vehicle for streams of emotional transformations. Therapy seems to do this a little at a time, in small doses, art more all at once, in greater leaps—but this may be an illusion. The totality of a work of art betrays an excruciating finitude of processes.

By totality I mean the more nearly complete way art portrays feeling. For example, murderous rage. Feelings you would not ordinarily bring to ultimate conclusion are standard literary fare. Parents, children, siblings, lovers: everyone killing everyone else and themselves. How telling that in drama the murder of strangers turns out to be a path to oneself, as if one could follow crumbs of cruelty home.

Yes, these things happen in real life. "Off with their heads," whether heads of state or rebels. Art doesn't invent murder, which, within and between nations, can be more horrible than anything art can portray. I've lived to see art overwhelmed by destructiveness it cannot keep up with, as it struggles to regroup, find new possibilities. In part, art portrays its own inability to digest the indigestible, the pain of failed processing.

Even so, we learn that the totality of what is imaginable does not work the way we imagine. If art teaches anything, it teaches that whatever emotion we invest in, the outcome is not as planned. Feelings sweep us and we follow them, but we remain novices when it comes to where they lead.

Art can aid emotional digestion, if we develop our capacity to use it. It feeds us images and stories about our concerns and brings to light possibilities of experience our lives obscure. For one thing, art provides the most graphic, persistent critique of murder throughout history. Not only does it portray all kinds of murder, it realistically and imaginatively elaborates motivation and consequences. It attends to and dissects qualities of destruction attendant to political calculation and personal rage. It dwells not merely on acts of murder, but also on what they make us think and feel as perpetrator, victim, or witness.

There is art that celebrates murder—Homer and King Arthur stories, for example, which bring out the honor, glory, and nobility of war, its attendant virtues of might, bravery, skill, sacrifice. Skill to kill. In Homer, at least, there is an appreciation for the swelling and ebbing of spirit and feeling, emotional tides tied to the rise and fall of fortune, coupled with grief over loss. In the radiance of heroes, nuclear madness is laid bare. Is it merely a contemporary read-back to find ironic humor in an erotic theft triggering years of social, military, and personal anguish and ruin, the vast combustibility of human affairs? Whether or not Homer meant this as a critique of human madness, the absurdity of solving blemish with rage opens a window on the weirdness of our plight. That murder fails to right things is a great discovery communicated and explored in art.

Murder is a kind of therapy. It attempts to remove the cause of what one feels is wrong. It tries to solve problems of pain, injustice, corruption by destroying sources of stain, impurity, unfairness. Art teaches, in great detail, that problems survive murder. Stain and inequity resurface, flaws continue. Not much is added to human knowledge by murderous solutions except, perhaps, growth of awareness that murder does not achieve (for long) the results it envisions. For humanity as a whole, murder is a delaying tactic, although it may seem so final.

One can read in Homer a sense of murderous rage as affliction, not merely as a link with glory. In the Bible, too, people rely too much on destruction to solve problems, which then regroup and multiply. Rage as cure is temporary. In Shakespeare, rage worsens problems it tries to solve or obliterate (e.g., Othello, Lear). I believe Hamlet unconsciously has difficulty with revenge because his sensibility intuits that righting things by murder is doomed. Indecision, in this context, represents potential growth of reflexivity, ability to symbolize. Of course Hamlet must kill to avenge his murdered father. But he knows the chain of murder wreaks havoc. He is not as immediately reactive as Lear or Othello, and the fact that tradition's code of honor is at stake makes his hesitation all the more valuable. It is inconceivable that Hamlet would not avenge his father's murder with murder, but the path to such cleansing is costly. The destructive path to purity is itself a gory stain. Part of Hamlet's despair is connected with sensing that the murder he must enact solves nothing. Hamlet's hesitation is a treasure he passes to us, the beginning of a different sort of ethic, in which hesitation opens nascent symbolic pathways. In the play, great art grows in indecision, an art of indecision, waiting in uncertainty as a new kind of freedom. The virtual celebration of indecision over war is aborted, overwhelmed by warrior urgency, but it is noted and transmitted.

Perhaps Christianity's fatal flaw is the centrality of a murder. Christianity crystallizes the ancient theme of death as solution, as purifier. The emphasis is on destroying death and sin, the transfiguration of murder. But death will never be destroyed by death; nor can the latter cleanse sin. Fight fire with fire, violence with violence: payback (Jesus as payment for the debt of sin), accounting and balance (psychospiritual balance by balancing accounts). Can one achieve wholeness in faith by mutilating faithless elements?

No solution based on murder solves the problem of human rage. Rage is always incorporated into one's Vision of the Good, my or our Good vs. yours. One of the most terrible facts of rage is its intimate allegiance with the sense of righteousness. Perhaps Christianity will have to stop murdering itself before it stops murdering others. The murdered God (as son), like Hamlet's father, must lead to further murders in the face of the will to forgive.

Now Islam tells us it wages holy wars. Murderous rage calls attention to sacred causes, redresses injury and neglect. A certain kind of rage to kill is sacred rage, holy wrath. Links between wrath, divinity, will, and injury come together.

Even child abusers justify themselves as trying to cure the young of troubles: "I was trying to get the devil out of her." Being on God's side is a dangerous business. Rage as an attempt to right things runs sickening risks. To complicate things, rage seems built into an infant's scream. Would the mother know something was wrong if the baby didn't scream? Yet this spontaneous tendency fuses with a sense of "right" as one gets older, and how much wrong this right engenders!

No book can pull the plug on rage. Rage is part of our condition, and we must learn to work with it. Psychotherapy tries to find ways to make room for ourselves. It is an experiment in uncertainty. In my view, hesitation plays a valuable role in the growth of self. Psychotherapy as an art of indecision provides a little balance to the decisiveness valued by the dominant culture. Attentive waiting can be restorative in its own right, while providing time and chance for feelings to be experienced, even digested. Hesitation opens alternative symbolic journeys.

The saying "He who hesitates is lost" has its applications. But what is lost by the totality of rage seems the greater danger. Rage, more than most states, affords a sense of totality, experiencing one's being with all one's might. A fit of rage provides an illusory sense of obstacles vanishing, euphoric boundlessness, even if one is in pain. For moments, rage that grows from pain obliterates pain. However, rage against pain readily translates to rage against self. It is no accident that some of the greatest ragers in history have ended as suicides (a tragic, often hideous "totality").

This book is a meditation on rage and pain and self. It works indirectly, informally, turning variations of rage over and over, considering them now from this angle, now from that. It is episodic, fragmentary, with inherent emotional rigor. The aim is gradual increment of experiencing. To experience rage rather than enact it opens places one could not have gotten to by blowing (oneself) up.

Rage has the strange characteristic of affirming life by obliterating it, traumatizing what it tries to open. Affirmation through obliteration is too injurious a coin for common emotional exchange, even if it is a language we all understand.

One day Devorah came into my office looking pinched, formless, collapsed. "It finally happened," she said. "Hell broke loose. The nightmare."

I took one look and without hesitating said, "Family. Family life."

"You knew—you knew." She nods, waits, sinks, pulls herself up a little. The past few months were good, maybe better than ever. She was saying things like, "I'm more myself, less intimidated, more like I've wanted to be. I can't believe it's happening."

Then her son's family came to stay for a month.

She was looking forward to it, an excited grandma, but dreaded losing time to herself. She was used to being able to walk, read, go to shows, write, just be. Now she was expected to be grandma, the baby-sitter.

No, it wasn't just baby-sitting. It was baby-loving, child-loving. The children weren't babies anymore.

The first seven days or so were OK. I think back over past visits. They begin well, end terribly, like clockwork. "You need to remember after a week or so, things fall apart. You're good for a week."

"Yes, ten days is about all I can take—all *we* can take. Gary, who loves doing things with the kids, breaks down too. He's impatient, screaming. Last night he let Sarah have it."

Gary is Devorah's husband, the grandfather, and Sarah is the daughter-in-law. "Sarah acts like we're slaves. She wasn't like that at first, but, as time went by, she became bossy. Now she's the big boss. She sleeps most of the day, gets up, meets friends, goes to events, and barks out orders. I feel badly for Lou. He takes it. He goes along with her, tries to smooth things over. It pains me to see this. Gary can't stand it." Lou is Devorah and Gary's son, a deep part of Devorah's heart.

"Gary blew."

"What happened?"

"Lou gave the kids a bath and Jill was dancing around with a towel around her, and they were watching TV. Then Sarah woke up and started screaming—what was Jill doing naked in a towel, why were they watching TV, ranting on and on. Gary blew and shut her up. 'You're sleeping half the time, yell the other half and don't know what's happening and expect others to take care of the kids and then can't take it when they do!' He lit into her.

"The kids wet their beds that night. The next day Sarah was quieter, but you could see it building and nothing would change."

Sarah was raised ultra-Orthodox Jewish, and she and Lou lived by the rules, although Lou was more relaxed about it. He liked his kids to have a good time and didn't bristle when his daughter wrapped herself in a towel after a bath and hung out. He didn't feel watching extra TV on vacation would ruin his children's Torah health. The Torah and life's sweetness went together for him.

And his wife's rage? Was she the local Jahveh? Was she God's fury?

Such deep contradictions run through life. Religious people— shouldn't they be loving? It was as if Sarah's religion was an excuse for rage.

I know I was being ungenerous as I sat and listened. It wasn't Judaism's fault that Sarah was self-indulgent. Self-indulgent? Again —ungenerous, inaccurate. Sarah usually was hard-working, devoted, caring. But she was also bossy and given to tantrums. She excused herself—she couldn't help it, this is the way she was, the way God made her. She simply went along with her nature, lived it, gave into it. She offered no resistance to herself. She did not struggle with her being.

Again—wrong, inaccurate. She struggled somewhat sometimes. Without any struggle at all, things would be even worse.

( *Golden Calf* : 7 )

Lou was sweet, forbearing, keeping peace in the family. His mother cringed inside, pained for him. His father wanted him to stand up to his wife, set things straight. Finally, Gary proved himself the greater God. The storm burst, and his rage was louder, stronger, more fierce and directed than Sarah's.

Did it cleanse the air? Did it right things? Gary and Devorah got sick and stayed in bed for a week after their son and his family left. Soon Sarah would be back to her Jahveh tricks—with no greater God to limit her.

Rage knows no boundaries. It sweeps across religions. But it is deep in the Jewish God I know and in those who love Him. Little Jahvehs everywhere, on street corners of New York, in teenage gangs, in synagogues, schools, sport arenas, and high offices. Jahveh fighting Jahveh—local gods vying for bragging rights, territory, a moment's omnipotence, boundlessness.

The flood recedes and things go back to normal, although kids continue to sleep in fetal positions and wet beds. Part of normal means rage will come again, suddenly, alarmingly—earth will be threatened, then the rainbow will come afterward for a time. Rage and rainbow, inextricably mixed.

Perhaps peaceful Lou and rageful Sarah are two parts of a system, each with functions. Lou can't be so innocent and Sarah so wrong, but what the ins and outs are I don't know. They are in family therapy, and things are better than they were. They are terribly caring, loving people. They will probably stay together for the rest of their lives, and one can only hope they will evolve. Growth is possible in nearly all circumstances, and these are far from the worst I've ever heard about.

Listening to Devorah, I got absorbed in my own fantasy. I pictured Moses bringing stony laws from God's lips, laws surely meant to rein in rage. If Sarah followed the Law, could she let herself go so easily?

There was no commandment, "Thou shalt not rage." But there were commandments to love God, respect parents, curb behavior and states of mind with regard to neighbors (don't murder, commit adultery, envy what others have). Can God give permission to take feelings out on children? On those closest?

I think of Freud's writing on Michelangelo's *Moses,* the intensity of mind, spirit, and body, pressure exerted against rage. For the moment, all-out war on rage, rage against rage. We have an urge to transcend ourselves, a need not simply to give in to the lowest denominator. Does law try to fill the gap when the drive to transcend ourselves weakens?

Law is ennobling. But rabbis say Moses had a problem with rage and could not enter the Promised Land because of it. Perhaps his brother, Aaron, the peacemaker, had a problem with meekness. Again, counterparts, like Sarah and Lou. Even the lawgiver has lawless moments.

Perhaps lawless moments follow higher, lower, or other laws.

Sarah's lawlessness, giving in to a blinding surge. What is it? Can we take it apart, see how it works? Can we expect her to try to hold it back, as Moses often did and sometimes didn't?

I've never met Sarah, so cannot know. I speak only from the Sarah in my mind, one planted by Devorah, matching something in my nature.

What happens in the red or white flash, the moment when one cannot wait? Sarah awakens, hears sounds, laughter, nonsense, people enjoying themselves—TV, a godless business. She is groggy, stumbles out of the bedroom, sees her daughter's nakedness wrapped in a towel—that is, sees nakedness in her mind, raw imaginings, inflammatory images. Her family dances around the golden calf. She is Moses bringing the Law. Her flare-up breaks people rather than tablets.

Rage cuts revelers in half, quarters, pieces of all sorts. At once, laser sharpness and shotgun splatter. It rushes through bodies, which contract, freeze, strike back, while numb eyes stare in disbelief.

TV is the golden calf. Laughter is the golden calf. A girl's naked body wrapped in a towel is the golden calf.

What enables a person to feel so right, to let oneself go, to inflict psychic fluids on others (rage = furious orgasm, spittle, psychic blood pouring out, turning to ice)? In this case, one splatters those closest to one, one's very own, those one almost feels to be oneself.

I am a jealous God. You must have no other gods. The I or self gets mixed with this.

Is there always megalomania in rage? Animals can be goaded to rage, and sometimes rage spontaneously for the hell of it. Rage may be expressive of primal energy, a baby's scream, a sun's explosion. Explosive processes are part of our universe. Do we know how to evaluate rage? Can we learn?

Yet something in me and Gary and Devorah says Sarah's rage is wrongly wounding, misplaced, in fundamental error. It interrupts and ruins good moments. But is it really blind? Is blind rage a seeing rage?

The pop—white, black, red flash—what does it see and think and feel? What does it stop? What does it hide?

Rage substitutes for growth, fills holes in self, masks deficiencies. It is allied with a sense of helplessness, disability, frailty. It hammers others into helplessness. Sarah's rage is a showstopper. It freezes others' spontaneity, immobilizes and attempts to control others. It tries to squeeze reality into one's own narrow frame of reference.

A baby screams when beset by trouble. It lacks a frame of reference for mounting discomfort, pain, hunger, thermal changes, waves of circulatory sensations, irritating wetness, frightening images, sights, sounds, and "feels." A scream mixes rage with terror to offset the latter. It can be blindly reactive yet have communicative value, attracting help, seeking change. Screaming expresses fear and helplessness and makes one feel stronger. It can express a sense of primal might and effort. Mixtures of terror and rage also go beyond what we can articulate.

Rage can lead to change. It can force others to hear that something is wrong, call attention to oneself or one's cause, stimulate the need to help. Rageful cries of pain sometimes have social value. Noise attracts notice and makes aspects of one's state visible to others.

But Sarah is a grown-up. Her rageful cry for help is at her children's expense. She blots out deficiency and helplessness by paralyzing others. She is at the point in life where she should be dealing with her outrage, not simply inflicting it on others. At the same time, she needs a place—like therapy—where screams can gain a hearing.

Why therapy, not simply life? Because she goes on screaming in life to no avail. She blots out the self-protective responses of others. Those near her do their best to survive. Their distress does not get through to her. She is not deeply changed by what she does to others. Yet she sees the pain she inflicts out of the corner of her eye and feels badly too, but she cannot stop. It would be worse if she did not see and felt no pain at all.

She blows up—explodes. We need to keep meditating on our explosive capacity. We've made beginnings—religion, philosophy, psychology, literature, art—multimillennial meditations on processes that make us up. We need to keep picturing what we imagine these processes to be, talking about them, turning them this way and that.

Rage is part of social justice, the urge to right inequity and abuse. But it is also part of abuse and continues the affliction. It runs deep in all directions, allied with righteousness and cruelty, dominance-subservience, freedom-slavery.

We think we understand that a baby cries when distressed and that the cry is meant to make things better. We cannot avoid mixing fantasy, observation, interpretation, and we think that screams are meant to right a wrong, that rage is part of an elemental attempt to right things. Perhaps this elemental response is with us all life long and transfers to events that cause distress or difficulty.

The poet teaches that we rage against death as well as life, death as a great affront, an injury to life, an injustice, a wrong.

What image of wrong beset Sarah, one wonders? Whatever was she thinking when she stumbled out of bed and saw/imagined things were not as they ought to be? What violation called forth rage? Was it real or imaginary violation?

( *Golden Calf* : 11 )

Gary surely put his finger on something by saying that others cared perfectly well for her children while she neglected them. Perhaps "neglect" is too strong. While she took time off on vacation, let go of control, others filled in nicely. Did she feel guilty for taking time, sleeping, letting her kids go? Did she imagine she was burdening others, that she was shirking? Did rage partly drown out guilt?

Perhaps Sarah's rage goes back to a time when she squeezed into a personality that worked for Orthodox Judaism, rigidly conceived. She was subject to massive dos and don'ts, superstition (if you step on a discarded fingernail fragment when pregnant, you are subject to miscarriage), tightly organized rules. If you can die or lose a limb or a baby for not following a smaller rule, what might happen for disobeying a big one? God may forgive, but what price one pays with fear. One never knows when God's rage will beat out compassion.

Lou seemed to embody God's kinder side. Humble, caring, mild. Didn't he squeeze into the same system as Sarah? Actually, he was raised by secular parents with much more freedom. It wasn't until college that God struck him. He turned to Judaism out of love. Laws were lifelines from God, ways of uniting with Him, mystical vehicles. He felt released by Judaic laws because he clung to the numinous center they radiated from. To be bound by law is to be bonded to God, and lovers shiver as they get closer.

Lou spent a lot of time studying and teaching the Torah. He helped at home, but the major burden fell on Sarah to take care of the kids and find ways to do her own creative work. No wonder she spent time on vacation collapsing in bed. No wonder she was angry. She had to fight for every inch of freedom she could manage, while her husband flew through life in mystical ecstasy.

There are always milder and angrier people in any social system. Orthodox Judaism is no exception. We can speak of genetics, circumstance, temperament, division of sociopsychological labor, aspects of the psychic body. Compassionate and furious God. His Christian son, Jesus, is also humble and angry, passing on the rage-love gene. We do not really know how to conceptualize differences and variability, although we take some pretty good cuts at it. We put tags on what we see and feel, and trace their tracks through history.

Sarah was the rager in her family, Gary the rager in his. Sometimes rager meets rager and explosions reach new peaks.

Am I supposing Sarah is victimized by the system, by Lou's meekness? Is rage her way of being free or dominant or feeling strong?

Is rage always going to be part of contraction, a reaction to feeling pinched, puffing out to shatter a sense of shrinking? Is it always tied to a sense of injustice?

My feeling is that the answer is yes, but there is more. Rage is not a simple state or simply a matter of gender. Boy and girl babies scream. Men and women rage. Perhaps there was a time (now? still?) when men ragers outnumbered women ragers, but my clinical impression over forty years is that the sexes are neck and neck.

After factoring out social, sexual, and religious inequity (which one cannot do), there is still primal rage and more to study. In fact, social, gender, familial, and religious pressures can serve as a natural laboratory enabling us to look into the face of rage and say what we see or imagine.

Yes, Sarah's rage grows out of squeezing herself into a personality that meets gender, familial, social, and religious requirements. But it may also be that rage was there first and flowed into these settings, which inflamed rather than requited it.

Rage is inserted into settings that mold it, for example, over- or underplay it, fuse it with a variety of attitudes, feelings, cognitive frames, social possibilities. How lucky a raging child who meets a person who discerningly responds, someone who senses, intuits the pain, the complaint, the demand for righting things, the need for healing. For an infant, body pain gets translated into soul pain and vice versa. This confusion in infancy can translate into lifelong somatic difficulties and/or denial of feelings.

( *Golden Calf* : 13 )

A parent who ignores, indulges, angrily silences or otherwise breaks down in the face of baby rage sets the stage for outbursts like Sarah's, a mild outcome compared to what can happen. Rage becomes part of a way of life, something one may not like but takes for granted. It is seen as part of one's equipment, who one is, even if one sometimes wonders if this is who one must be.

Over time one gets used to being a semirageful person and responses that might have helped in infancy will no longer do the trick. No amount of understanding, caring, devotion, insight will make the rage go away or make one another kind of person. A version of what one might have been hardens, dominates, rigidifies —one has become a rageful being.

A precise logic works in relationships. Sarah, a rageful being, finds a man who will endure her. She gravitated toward a gentle, kindly soul who put up with her. Life would have been even more hellish had she picked or been picked by another rager, which often happens. As a chronic rager, Sarah was a bit like Lou's father. In some sense, Lou found aspects of his father in female form.

It may be that Lou was addicted to rage or needed it in his life. Perhaps he tried, through Sarah, to get something he needed from his father. Maybe he was trying to get past traumatizing rage to deeper acceptance and mutual recognition. He picked someone whose rage he hoped would turn to goodness, while his own mild persona and godly love at once slaked and fueled the fire.

Once chronic reactive patterns solidify, they become a mold around the self. Self is trapped by reactions it is prone to. I believe Sarah when she says she cannot help herself, she is what she is, although she wishes she were different.

At the same time, she feels her rage is justified, that she is right. To my mind, what justifies it and keeps it going is not simply the current situation, but moments lost in history. After all, to cause so much damage in a moment's outburst—an outburst that repeats over time—really, did her daughter deserve that? Should her daughter pay for imaginary transgression with sudden, alarming laceration? Must injustice inflicted on Sarah sear her daughter?

Reactive patterns, once established, are hard to change. What can therapy do? I think someone like Sarah needs awakening to the damage she causes loved ones, and the damage she causes herself. Without a perception of how damaging rage is, there is little reason to change. The sense of damage must be acute, heartfelt. In ancient times, one rended garments in grief over the death of a loved one or in response to awareness of one's sins. What is needed in Sarah's case is a rending of soul that recoils in horror upon seeing what rage does. And that soul must seek help.

One must truly feel the pain rage inflicts, and the pain of one's own life as well. Therapy helps focus where the pain is in one's life and the effects of that pain on others. One learns, over time, to speak from the pain place and go beyond it, to hear the pain of others and develop resources in the face of it. I don't think, for someone like Sarah, that short-term therapy will do. She is going to need repeated chances, little by little, to find places in herself she long ago gave up on. She is going to have to meet the wound in rage's center.

What could possibly get her attention, if the pain she causes her children goes undigested, if she shrugs it off with an obliviousness similar to that of those who injured her?

"Tell Sarah that she is the golden calf," I say to Devorah. "And she worships the golden calf."

"I couldn't do that. It would make things worse. It would cause an explosion she'd never get over. She'd be so hurt things would never be the same. It would take years for us to be ok again. She'd stop talking to me."

Sarah must have seen her daughter (wrapped in towel, watching TV) dancing around the golden calf. She, Sarah, rages against sin. She is on God's side. Mind reverses subject-object and subject-subject. Sarah herself is the golden calf and the calf's worshipper (whoreship?). Not simply rage addict, but rage worshipper. Here rage and self are one.

Am I right? nuts? constructive? destructive? Should I keep thoughts like this to myself, wait and see?

( *Golden Calf* : 15 )

"No, no," says Devorah. "I couldn't do that."

But she believes what I'm saying, sees it, a kind of lucid truth, a truth she fears would harm.

"If Sarah were here right now, I'd call her a golden calf," I perversely persist, my rascal mind. I feel an evil smile spread inside my heart, as well as on my face.

Devorah is smiling too.

Psychotics speak of nerve rays and radioactive waves as forces of influence in daily life. They see or fear waves or rays streaming from others or themselves, taking over personality, threatening spirit.

This language of vision is by no means limited to the clinically mad. The psychical realities involved are no less compelling to many individuals who glimpse the rage of injury and illumination.

Soren speaks of radioactive containers in the basement of his college. They are in suitcases. He fears they will leak. They come from physics experiments. The authorities keep them a secret but everyone knows. The kids in class try to be oblivious but are in danger of being poisoned. Soren is a tenured professor of literature. Perhaps his imagination is overactive. He fears poisoning his students, wanting to nourish them. He feels driven to open all the inner radioactive containers he can find—in himself, in everyone.

He has a compelling urge to put his penis in a baby's mouth. After a time I ask him to be the baby, and he sees himself gripping his mother's nipple and it is all radioactive—the nipple, the milk. He is the radioactive mother with his students.

Soren feels damaged beyond repair, compelled toward a damaging feed in order to heal and perpetuate the damage. Cruel circle, trying to heal illness by perpetuating it, perpetuating it to heal.

The danger is the spread of radioactivity. Radioactive rage everywhere. How long do containers hold?

Is fellatio a container, a soother? Licking wounds? Making better?

The mouth is a funny kind of container, funnel, first stop toward digestion. It contains the evaluating tongue—how does it taste? good? bad? A snake in the cave of the garden of good and evil. Tongues can be wrong. Poisons can be doctored to taste good. One can kill oneself following taste.

Digestion begins with the eyes; hands follow eyes; later, hands, feet, and genitals follow and lead. Take in, spit out? Moments of truth.

Is Soren's urge to put his penis in a baby's mouth an attempt at self-repair? a compulsion to inflict damage, perpetuate trauma? He is the big one now, the mamanipple, radioactive medium, life stopper in the guise of giver.

Is there urge to put a penis in any opening that will envelop it? Fantasies of bursting baby open with a bayonet, a bomb exploding baby from within. Milk of life. God-Mom gives and takes away.

Soren has a great need to feel guilty, a need to convert anxiety to guilt. Nipple-penis God-Mom, attractor, organizer for anxiety-guilt running amok, chaotic radioactive particles throughout the psychic universe. Perhaps he is trying to lick his wounds, to fix what hurts.

Is it possible to locate what hurts? Where will the finger point? "I hurt all over," comes the reply. "In my heart, my chest, my gut, my eyes, joints, back, my——." Where is this hurt? Can anyone find it?

Rage cocoons this ache. Secondary aches cocoon this rage.

Look what people do or want to do to make it better. Penises in baby's mouths in one or another form.

Often wounds are obvious, but often—Soren tries to say this— they proliferate under cover of being nourishing. To put his penis in a baby's mouth as a gesture of nourishment, repair, trauma. Being big at someone's expense, loving self through another's littleness, passing damage to the next generation. The rage of trauma inducts each generation. Wound, rage, healing leading to further wounding.

Soren tries to nourish himself by traumatizing himself. The infant he traumatizes is himself as well as a possible other. If he enacts his fantasy, he will never recover from guilt, which will be passed to the next generation. In such a case, self-nourishment and self-traumatization are identical and persist through time.

I look at Soren and for an instant see fellatio as part of human contact. Did it take psychoanalysis to discover an area of unconscious nipple-penis identity, fusion of both with mouth, sucking, nourishment, enfolding and penetrating love? Nipple and penis are parts of a larger category that W. R. Bion calls "links" and of which he says, "The earliest problems demanding solution are related to a link between two personalities." So many oral links are fused with toxins: smoking, drinking, talking. We not only get rid of poisons, but also create poisons (as well as nourishment) through speech. Too often milk and shit are one. But milk alone may have toxins, and emotions are at once nourishing and poisonous.

There is a sucking dimension in human contact. We may suck each other off or dry in a pejorative sense or try to make each other feel good by catering to narcissism. But there are deeper currents, in which the possibility of nourishing and being nourished holds sway. To nurse and be nursed leaves a very deep template. Terms like "blow job" or "getting sucked off" fuse a more hostile current with the wish for nourishment and healing. Always the hope, pleasure will wash away pain, imaginary dominance (control of the controller) will fill a gap.

There are passive needs, but how does one get to passivity in such an active age? Through collapse? getting blown away? some kind of addiction? imaginary absorption through mucous membranes? To lie there and be taken care of and become a filament of living tissue, doesn't one need a semi-active partner? Does Soren reverse roles, turning the passive active, becoming the fantasy doer? Can one be passive only if one is traumatized—only to become, in turn, another active traumatizer?

Radioactive breast, food, nipple, sucking as part of relationship, mutual sucking, one at a time. Dogs lapping, cats licking, tongues, membranes, liquids, emotional porousness. Is Soren saying I am putting my penis in his mouth or that baby me makes him feel big?

( *Radioactive Waves* : 19 )

Who is making who feel big and/or little? Analysis is too exciting: more pleasure in therapy than one can stand.

Is therapy a kind of blow job? Who's blowing whom? It keeps reversing, becomes interchangeable, with pressure to make it one way or the other. Who is the bigger baby bidding for narcissistic repair? Therapist, patient—licking wounds.

# MORE
## RADIOACTIVITY,
## LICKING, BEATING,
## CHEWING

Can one lick rage away?
A little while?
A little while more?

———

To build capacity to lick wounds well is no small thing.

———

Licking chops, skin, genitals.
Getting one's licks in.
Getting a licking, licking (beating) someone.

———

The conjunction of caring and hostility runs deep. Karl Abraham spoke of an oral sucking and oral biting stage. Analysts thought biting was the snake in the garden. If only biting didn't hurt, mother would not wince. If only the breast would not feel pain, human beings would not feel guilty. If only God produced pain-free beings, there would be no holding back.

But there is the conjunction of nursing, caring, licking, and— biting/beating. As if helping and hurting go together. Dependency brings out protectiveness, love, and aggressiveness, the urge to push away, the need to make vulnerability wince, the need for space.

And beating? To be beat, lost, uncertain, unable to solve a problem. To lose. To injure, win, conquer. To get beaten at one's own game. If licking/liking/nursing/caring leads to beating, beating involves heart and pulse, rhythm (drumbeat), tempo. Breathing, heartbeat, this way, that, yes, no.

The waxing-waning of experiential surges—on, off.

As teeth develop, chewing slows one down. Rage gets channeled, if not digested. Still, one gets mad at oneself if one bites one's tongue or cheek by "mistake." Rage surges at the least provocation, at reminders of pain. It is difficult enough to avoid necessary pain at the hands of others. One imagines, at least, one ought not hurt oneself. But hurt oneself one does, in all kinds of ways, and rage at self mounts for flaws in omnipotence. Even chewing food can result in pain. One tries to be more careful for a while, but rage-prone omnipotence gets triggered by one thing or another.

One licks the rawness of the cheek's underside. The bitten tongue tries to lick itself. We do care and are gentle and make gestures of reparation. We soothe. But again we bite ourselves, soothing, seething. Such drama in the mouth.

The baby cries and laughs. Not just pain and pleasure—grief and joy. Doesn't mother need both? Doesn't baby?

Carrie says, "There's a ray. I see a ray shining in my head, through my head. A rageful ray. Very bright light, burning bright. It's been there for a long time, since I was a little girl, but I've tried not noticing it. I look away, close my inner eyes, but I'm not sure it's something inner. It's there, somewhere, I'm not sure where. I say to myself it's not real, it's imaginary. But I have to tell you it feels real and I'm starting to feel that it *is* real. The truth is it *is* real, but I don't know what to do with it and I've been afraid of it. I've been afraid of it all my life. It makes me feel I don't know what real is, and I'm beginning to think I don't.

"If this ray is real, then what *is* real?

"It gives me a surge of power. If I relax and watch it and it goes through me, I feel stronger. The ray races through my tissues, nerves, muscles, skin. I feel more alive. I'm tempted to pull up into my eyes and watch it. I think I've been watching it out of the corner of my eyes for a very long time. That's not accurate. It's always in the center of my vision. How come I don't see it most of the time? I go on with my life as if it isn't there. Now I want to say—and it is the truth—that it is always at the center of vision but I am able not to see it and go on as if it is not there.

"I can't tell whether it stays the same or whether I change in relation to it. I get bigger or smaller and let it flow through more or less of me or shut it out. It seems to stay the same size and brightness, but I'm not sure. If I let it flow through more of me, I feel stronger and happier. If I narrow my vision and look at it through an eye aperture, I feel curiosity and fear. I feel it can rip through me, tear me, burn me—it will damage me. I will never recover.

"I am damaged and ever recovering.

"I feel it is healing me. Is it damaging or healing?

"Most of my life I've organized it by being paranoid—it gets projectively organized. Maybe knowing I have you to fall back on enables me to let it go through my body. I was better with people this week, less hostile, less withdrawn. I had more energy. From the ray."

———————

"Rage radiation," says Alan. "It goes through me. Screaming radiation rage. Pumps up my chest, back, arm muscles. Coursing through my body. Ready to smash someone. I scream at my wife and kids. Not as much as I used to. You've helped me with that. But I do. It's still there. It's there now.

"What triggered it this time was getting a producer for my play. I've not gotten this far before. Maybe this time it'll go through. Maybe not." Alan has been trying to get one of his plays produced for years. He makes his living working with computers, but he's an unsuccessful writer.

"I mean, how good can this producer be if he's interested in me? He hasn't done much in years. He's out of fashion. What good can this do me? He'll probably fail or screw up. If I'm his major client, what kind of a producer can he be?"

Alan pauses. Laughs worriedly. I say, "Radioactive rage spoils a lot of potential good feeling."

"I do get a good feeling from him. When he told me he wanted to do it, I felt great. Then the rage came. Distrust. Spreading—radioactive poison—all through me, instead of the good feeling. It took the good feeling's place. I can't help it. It came over me.

"I can see now maybe it got triggered by mistrust. I'm used to being ignored, mistreated, lied to. I start thinking something's wrong if he's good to me. People don't return my calls or they break appointments. I'm expecting that. But he sounds happy to hear from me. He's looking for ways to do it, to find the right people for it. I don't want to build my hopes up. It's hard to keep a lid on. Flying high, waiting to crash. I get furious thinking it's a sham, it'll come to nothing, and I'll have been a fool to open myself to it. I hate myself for thinking it can happen. Rage obliterates hurt before it happens but it's based on hurt in the past. It spoils the moment, brakes joy—breaks joy. I know reality sucks—I know what the chances are. Yet I can't stop feeling—maybe this is it. I feel great, then the rage comes."

Rage obliterates hope, protects hope. Rage shields. Accuses.

Jeff has a good feeling about himself and life. He is keenly aware of life's permeating beauty. He married a woman who incarnated the beauty he felt, then began a descent from disappointment through hell to unknown territory. Through it all, Jeff never lost his sense of life's beauty, not for long, not completely.

If I speak of basic beauty, someone must say, "What of the ugliness, evil, injury to so many unfortunate beings? What of the ugliness of beauty? And what of the devil's beauty? Isn't the devil the most radiant of beings?"

Did Jeff love his wife? He loved her beauty. Did he know *her*? *Could* he know her?

Marriage is a gnostic journey. It takes one to new dimensions of uncertainty and drives one to a deeper apprehension of what knowledge can be. One must not underestimate gains that come from an ever growing education in futility. We learn about each other through what we are, perhaps even more through what we are not.

Begin with an elementary proposition, a disturbing reality, an awesomely inspiring-putrefying tendency: Jeff thought (*imaginary expectation*) his wife was what she seemed to be, what she seemed to him.

She was beauty.

Beauty's essence in real life.

She was thus object and source of faith. Let us call her Rose.

Here are some subpropositions, equally real:

1. As ideal object, Rose filled a hole. Perhaps many holes, or the Great Hole, with myriad byways. For one thing, she answered a yearning for beauty ideal and real. She filled a longing.

2. As ideal object, Rose creates a hole. As soon as she is seen, the hole is perceived. It is experienced as being filled. A moment before, it did not exist. Suddenly, it is everything meaningful, flashing from nowhere.

3. In the moment, beauty is all. Reflections about the source, truth, value of beauty hide as beauty approaches. Awareness of transience and suffering disappear in the greater light. Fulfillment grows, emptiness recedes. The only pain that stains consciousness is the beauty of beauty itself, a joyous pain. A pain drowning in pleasure. A pain we could not notice, except it adds to joy.

By the time they married, Jeff "knew" Rose's history, but he had no idea what it meant in real living. More truly, he had lots of "ideas"—but real living was yet to come. Rose was severely abused in childhood. She was violated sexually and was subject to other forms of violence. That she survived as well as she did is one of those tributes to the love that marks our souls.

Apparently she became as radiant as her injury was dark. Jeff was star-struck. As mentioned above, to look at her was to feel pained reverence, longing fulfilled. In the early days of their relationship, she was sexually alive. That died. As time revealed, her outer beauty had mysterious ties with profound depression.

Rose was a good mother and cared for her children and Jeff. But Jeff more and more felt something was missing—she was not there. It was not that she simply went through the motions. There was reason to believe that her love and good intentions were real. Whatever survived, she made the most of it. But Jeff was getting the horrifying realization that little survived, and what survived was seriously compromised.

Rose mobilized herself to create a world where disturbance might be minimized. She kept an even tone in the household, keeping excitement down. She viewed Jeff's love of feeling as crazy. Jeff thrived on intensity. Emotional nuances and extremes nourished him, or so he thought. Now and then Rose would say, "Do what you need to do. I don't have the kinds of feelings you want. I love you, though, and care and want you to be happy." Again, "I can't follow you to the places you need to go. I can't find them. I don't have them."

It may be that Rose associated emotional intensity with trauma and that traumatic intensity absorbed or stopped her natural affect flow. Thus strong emotion becomes a signifier of trauma and is somehow made to go away.

Her relationship to Jeff's hunger for affect was both mystified and split. On the one hand, his need for strong feeling was a voice from another world. She thought it crazy and treated him as an inane baby with an eccentricity to put up with. On the other hand, she realized people may need more feeling than she. Her friends criticize her for not being there for them. Since she has good will, this baffles her. She has come to think she must be lacking something others have, but there is nothing she can do about it. She may try to fill gaps by acting "normal," but those who want to be close to her become frustrated.

Writing this reminds me of something I said to Jeff near the end of our first session. "Today you let me know about the women in your life. Perhaps soon you will let me know about yourself." He was startled. Telling me about his women was telling me about himself. He took complaining about women for granted. *They* were his *problem,* and he wanted to know what made him choose them. He wanted to drink in beauty in deep, deep intimacy. It seemed like it ought to be the easiest thing in the world. What made it so difficult?

Jeff felt he came close to what he wanted with a former lover, Gwen. They drank in feeling with great gulps. She gave him heaven, also hell. He was ready to leave his wife for her, the promised land. But she broke up with him, told him he was too engulfing and she had to get away. She wanted to feel free. So did he. For him, their relationship was freeing: for her, getting out of it was more so.

He couldn't believe she didn't want him. "No one broke up with me before. I've always been the one to end it."

Jeff spoke about the breakup for months. "How could she throw something so beautiful away?" he asked. "So near, so far," I said. "As close as I've ever gotten," he said.

He couldn't take in the fact that it wasn't the same for Gwen. "I don't need you for emotional intensity," she told him, trying to release him. "The heavens and hells you speak of—that's the way I am." She is like this with others, like this with herself.

Gwen, like Rose, came from a highly traumatized background. Rose shut off emotional extremes in order to survive the tumult. Gwen couldn't stop plunging in, fighting fire with fire. She was both neglected and scorched by adult thunder, an emotional diet of rage and emptiness. She was brought up by stormy, self-centered yet desperately deprived and depriving people and foraged for nourishment amidst outbursts and withdrawal. In Rose, Jeff found an emotional crater, in Gwen a volcano.

Were Rose-Gwen soul mirrors of minimum-maximum emotion, Jeff's proxies?

Both women did well at work. Rose ordered her life to balance work and family. Gwen went from man to man but had a brilliant career, oriented around herself. Apparently trauma energizes as well as skews and results in different "solutions."

Jeff did not understand why he was drawn to deeply traumatized women. It seemed an accident of fate, not anything to do with him. Were there more traumatized people than others in the pool? If most were traumatized, the luck of the draw was weighted. Jeff did not feel especially traumatized himself. He felt generally OK about himself and his feelings about life. He felt capable of uniting pleasure with stability and envisioned a soul mate with whom to explore the nuances of intimacy. Why such wounded women?

Where was Jeff's trauma?

Lost in the celebration of his life?

Little by little I hear of strangulated elements. Jeff's father was successful but secretive, at once generous and stingy. As a man who once was poor, then wealthy, he was suspicious, fearful, guarded. He emphasized form over substance—good manners, dress, appearance, finely polished surfaces. He was more interested in how Jeff looked than in how he felt. Jeff did not feel wealth made his father this way, but it helped. Still, his father was industrious, and Jeff grew up in a world where work was important. He thus felt given to, as well as stifled.

Jeff's mother was quiet, critical, elegant, yet she sometimes lapsed into primordial grossness, as we will see. In a way, his parents gave Jeff lots of room, as long as he looked the part, that is, looked good. He felt stifled more by his father than his mother, although his father was away at business much of the time. The family was shaped by his father's rhythms, values, wishes. His mother seemed more a stand-in for his father's wishes in his father's absence, rather than pressed by her own desires. His father's earning power expressed a strength in the face of which the family gave way. He pictured his mother quietly standing in the shadows, the balance of power lopsided.

What didn't fit the frame was that Jeff sensed his father's spirit sag. A spiritual sag marked the background of his father's being, which Jeff fought off. From a very early time, he saw something crushed in his father, which success offset but could not undo. Something in his father was determined to rise above early damage and did, but the damage did not go unnoticed by his child.

Jeff refused to be stifled by damage in his father or by his mother's emptiness. He refused to be damaged. He spent a lot of time talking about how OK he was compared to people in his life. Then, during a session, I became aware that I was breathing and he was not. When I asked him about this he said, offhandedly, that yes, he was aware of how shallow his breathing was. He always was a shallow breather. Where was his breath coming from? not his belly or chest? his neck? It is impossible to breathe simply with a head, like a vapor, yet this is close to what it seemed like.

He seemed to feel that not breathing might enable him to live longer.

Casually, Jeff mentioned respiratory problems since childhood—asthma, allergies—as well as intestinal difficulties, mostly controlled by medication. He tolerated them as physiological weaknesses but did not let them affect his basic good feeling. He fought off the notion that his problems might have anything to do with emotional air and nutrients. It would be some time before he could feel any hint of terror at having too little or too much emotional air, improper or insufficient emotional nutrients. Is it possible to live one's life feeling good yet unconsciously caught between being unable to breathe and starving to death? A time will come when Jeff sees himself (as infant, child) in danger of being sucked up by a collapsed pocket of his father's psyche, gasping for breath as his mother disappears into thin air. But for many years, Jeff would not be dragged down by his parents—he would not be crushed or empty. He would be fully alive.

And fully alive he was.

He was a top student, athlete, and musician from grade school through high school, after which he went to a top college. He had friends, girl friends, a good life. Eventually, he became a painter, lucked out in investments, and supported his art. He seemed to have a golden touch through his twenties, into his thirties, forties fast approaching. Girl after girl, painting after painting, so many good feelings.

His paintings failed to achieve the success he would like. He could not tell whether the problem was talent or marketing or both. He was not persistent or clever enough in making and sustaining the effort and contacts that marketing required. Was it a matter of energy, drive, ability? Now and then he would get moving, hit an invisible point, then draw back, as if the force of the wave would take him so far, and no further.

In time, he felt something similar at work in the act of painting itself. He would feel himself get to a certain point, then draw back, as if the work collapsed under him, and would go no further. If he waited or pushed, the work would continue. But what he hoped for didn't quite happen. He would end up with a good piece—but not something *better.*

For many years, Jeff didn't notice that the *other* thing, the *better* thing, wasn't happening. It wasn't an issue. He was swept up in the process, the joy of discovering himself, the joy of discovering *painting.* He had a good feeling about what he did, just as he had good feelings with women he saw. Painting was part of the glow of life. It can takes years to grow into a life, to begin to *see.* The apple of knowledge is not eaten all at once but a bite at a time.

In time, Rose became the apple of his eye, and he married. He had no reason to think things would not be good. He had a small investment firm which did well, possibly not as well as it might have if he gave himself to it more fully—but well enough. His inner clock told him it was time to have a family. He loved being a father, loved his kids, and sought help when he began to fear something in his attitude might harm them.

His sense that his painting wasn't good enough, that Rose wasn't good enough, spread to his children—they weren't good enough either. This horrified him because he thought they were wonderful. He loved them totally and enjoyed their very being. But if they didn't play the way he liked, if they didn't like what he imagined they should, if they liked malls rather than reading or art or sports—he felt himself coldly pressure them. He had pictures in his mind of what children should be like, not exactly his father's pictures perhaps, but his own version of icy control.

Control-collapse: Jeff was not yet ready to connect them.

He felt his critical bent justified with his wife. She was lax, spaced out, unavailable for ecstatic communion, yet (he had to begrudgingly admit) competent in her own unmeticulous way. She periodically had sex with Jeff, but vanished in the act (like his mother?). In truth, he was furious with her. His critical control masked and gave precision to what amounted to a chronic underpinning of long, drawn-out rage. It did not occur to him he might be injuring her. She already was deeply injured. And the fact that she was damaged grated on him and inured him to his ability to hurt her. He was bothered less by anything she did or didn't do than by her failure to be more alive. After all, he ought to have someone who could match his capacity to live, and his wife's way of living could not match his own. The quiet, even atmosphere she managed to produce was for him an infuriating deprivation.

To put down his wife was one thing. He felt legitimately disappointed, engaged in struggle. To put down his children was unconscionable. He knew it wrong to feel righteous if they failed his idea of them.

Jeff did things the right way. If he and Rose cooked, she would be sloppy, he precise. If they repaired a chair, she would make do, he would overdo. If they cleaned the house, his area sparkled, hers might be a little better than it had been. He could order tickets for a show and find his way there better than she. He must have been infuriating to live with. He pressured Rose to believe that her way was wrong, and he was sure she did the same with him. His children choked on their semisuppressed fury, in danger of being emotionally poisoned. Good as they were, their difficulties grew.

His children began waking with night terrors and their work in school suffered. Jeff tried to soothe their fears, but terror is a stubborn fact. Medication took the edge off his wife's fears, and his former girlfriend, Gwen, was used to living with dread (it didn't slow her down). But his children? What was he doing to them? Were they feeling some of the terror that eluded him?

Jeff felt too OK to be dragged down by faulty people around him. He wanted to know why an OK person like him didn't have OK people in his life. He knew they must exist—how could he find them? The mantra of OKness felt like a nail he was driving into me. There must be OK therapists to help clients find OK people—life enhanced by the winner within. Was I the wrong therapist (like wrong wife or child)? His trauma-free scenario slid off me, like trauma slid off him. Weren't the traumatized people close to him (including me) something other than choices to correct? Didn't they say something about his being? I know people so focused on

trauma there is no room for living. There must be something between sinking into trauma and the wish for Teflon victory.

"Do you pick women you can feel superior to?" I asked. I felt a
mixture of fear and hardness in my eyes, terror and persistence.
"Contempt is frozen terror," I said. "I don't feel terror," said Jeff.
"But I see it in those around me. I've acted above it but don't really
feel it in myself. Perhaps it's partly frozen. Maybe superiority is
cauterized terror, but I'm a long way from feeling it."

Jeff was caught between sympathy and superiority, although for
him the former could be a vehicle for the latter. He mostly told me
what was wrong with other people, and I began wondering if such
quietly careful, chronic criticalness smothered rage and terror with
sympathetic superiority.

Good feeling is good to have. But there is such a thing as idealizing one's own aliveness at the expense of others and at one's own
expense too. Good feeling blots out trauma, or comes through
in spite of trauma, or even incorporates trauma. But there can be
something cruel about good feeling that detracts from the ability
to taste another's pain, and one's own.

As time went on, Jeff felt more alone in his marriage than ever.
"I never thought being married meant being more alone than being single. You marry someone and you think there will be deep
intimacy. Instead you discover you live in different worlds and you
don't fit together the way you thought you would. You are different
kinds of people." Jeff thought of leaving Rose and might have, if
Gwen had wanted him. He stayed because of love for the children.
"My loneliness with Rose is excruciating, but I couldn't bear living
without the kids."

He began to notice changes in himself. "I don't think I wanted
to feel how painful my marriage was and covered by thinking it
should be different. *She* was the one who should change. *She* was
the one ruining things. *I* was waiting for her to come around and
be the person I married. *I* was waiting for her to become the person I knew she could be.

"I couldn't take in what was missing. I couldn't really let in the

( *White Rage of Beauty* : 33 )

fact that our marriage wasn't what I wanted it to be. I tried to make it something else. Deep down I was enraged. Outside I was calm, the better one, the one who knew joy. I couldn't let in that something was really missing in my life. I wanted it to be whole, complete. If I try to find wholeness through another partner, I'd miss my kids. My life would be torn without them. If I stay, I miss wholeness. It's not a position I expected—it's not what I envisioned."

Is it only a matter of realizing life is not what one imagined, not what one hoped? Trauma everywhere—wife, girlfriend, kids, parents, therapist. Jeff's coating of self-idealization and life-idealization was thick. The acid of trauma had a hard time eating its way in. Perhaps one day he would discover inexpressible trauma inside the heart of the idealizing coat, slowly eating its way out.

A few months later, Jeff could say there was something freeing about his newly growing aloneness. It was not only painful. He felt more himself through it. There were nuances of self-feeling he would have missed had he stayed so fixed on getting more from Rose. From the alone center, he could see more clearly how enraged he was and discover that his rage glued him to the need to make the other different. If rage were successful in obliterating the realness of the other, there would be no otherness at all, only a fantasy object fulfilling his beatific vision. Rose's depression forced Jeff to be more real.

Once he told me, "I've been staring at white rage flaring from nowhere. It comes from my wish for Rose to be what I want her to be. It is a link with Rose, a last link, keeping me attached in an old way. It stops me from growing, and although I feel I am my rage, it stops me from being me.

"All this time I thought it *was* me, the angry me at something missing. I didn't know I was so rageful. Mr. Nice Guy, a loving man. Some of the rage is part of clinging melded with control. I see a me I don't want to be, forcing others to be versions of what I want them to be. I had no idea I was this bad a tyrant. But it's not all I am.

"I've always been a seeker of beauty and never dreamt so much rage could be tied to love of beauty or that the way I relate to beauty could be so destructive. I don't know what to do with myself. I can't make myself disappear. Love and rage are fused. White rage keeps things the same, fuels my relationship to my wife, my imaginary wife. White rage keeps my relationship with my wife going. Life throws me back on myself. I couldn't stay with how alone I felt without raging it away. You're helping me stay there so I can see and feel."

Letting go of rage means letting go of his picture of marriage. Rage is partly a special hope for intimacy. White rage of beauty— disappointed again. Jeff is far from experiencing trauma around him as something in him.

We are now in our second year of work. Whiffs of bad feeling, the other side of idealization, come his way. "I had a weird fantasy the other day," Jeff says. "I pictured myself being born and felt gotten rid of. Don't you think that's odd, to feel unwanted because I couldn't stay in the womb? It's like I want to be in someone forever. To be born is to be unwanted, kicked out. Birth should mean starting, but that's not what I feel now.

"I'm brought back to a sick scene with my mother, seeing her take out and throw away her bloody tampax. Bloody baby, bloody soul, bloody rage. I feel thrown out like the bloody tampax, dispensable."

Jeff gets a hint of not feeling wanted. But he was adored. Where does not feeling wanted come from?

He begins to feel a discrepancy between his idolized self and other aspects of aliveness. To be idolized is wonderful but blots out self as much as rage does. To dip into self is to taste the world of the tear. Self produces rage and idolization to blur how badly self is torn.

Who was adored? Jeff's restrained, critical yet primitive mother, and hard-working, appearance-oriented father—how much of Jeff did they see, how much was included in the adoration process? Who was the Jeff who got left behind, banished from the kingdom, left outside the city walls to die? Slow-baking trauma, skewing a life toward self-idolization, leaving oneself out. Many feel left out of their own lives, at once included and excluded from their own beings.

Psychoanalysis, like religion, tells us how torn we are. But seeing this and making room for it are two different things. We produce states of being to fill tears, like mortar, but pain seeps through. Rage and idolization, twin fillers. Our means of healing ourselves makes us worse. If idolization and rage die down, what will Jeff find?

"I've been thinking of control all weekend. I've been seeing the Sistine Chapel in my mind. How's that for control? Picturing myself the creator, molding people. What an incredible idea! What an incredible need—to be the creator and control and define the shape others take.

"The truth is my life took the shape *it* wanted. It was richer because I could *not* control it. The creator-control idea robs you from yourself, steals others too. Yet there it is—I really have it. Something in me goes for it big-time."

While I listened to Jeff, I began thinking of "free will." Something about emphasis on will always seemed superficial to me. Now I appreciated it in a new way. All the friction, differences between people—so many in my lifetime streaked through my mind. Free will saves God from his omnipotence, saves us from omnipotence too. Friction saves us from ourselves. But can we save ourselves and each other from our necessary friction? Will it still be effective if it is less violent, mean, cruel?

Jeff was talking about a new woman on the horizon. "Part of what makes Paula attractive is that she's not porous. She's hungry, but has boundaries."

"Boundless hunger in a bounded frame," I say abstractedly, tuning in.

"Yes, perfect. That's exactly what I'm looking for. But it brings up something, a way I've always been. I've never been attracted to so-called feminine women. I've needed women who were more phallic. Oddly, my wife is drop-dead beautiful but tells me she's more male than female, and I believe her. She says her psychology is male—and she's right. Hardness protects me from the curves. Gwen was straight lines physically, emotionally's another question.

"Sex has played such a big role in my life. I really love sex. It's hard to get my mind around it, but this might be the first time I get a sense of how deeply threatened I am by sex. Yes, I love it. It's like standing on the edge and surviving. I think that's part of why I like it so much. It's a safe and wonderful thing to feel danger in, to jump and survive. It's like surfing in an ocean. Part of the joy is a wave can throw you over, dash you, and you hit bottom, go under and up and breathe again, rubbing your sore spots.

"I've complained a lot about what women have not brought into my life. Yet what did I look for? Hard women with edges. My wife is more of a survivor than anyone I know. She can get through any trauma but can't share soft emotion. She says the kinds of feelings I treasure have little relevance for her. She's very practical.

"It's coming to me that I'm really terrified of women. Can that be true? Is my mind making it up? Right now I really feel terrified of women. This cuts against the grain of my whole life, all the sex; my best friends have been women. Yet my women friends and sex partners, with psyches or bodies like erections, have been foils against the terror. It's very powerful, what I'm seeing and feeling now."

Does Jeff's need for hardness result from trauma, protect against trauma, induce more trauma?

"I'm soft and hard," he goes on. "I want women to share my soft feelings, but there's something cold in me, like Gwen's ability to detach while she's emotionally turbulent. Attachment and detachment. Coldness and warmth, hardness and softness, are simultaneous. How can I be cold and warm at the same time? But you know, I am. I could care less, yet have soft feelings. Of course, sometimes I do care, but I'm not sure how often or how much.

"I feel something monstrous in me, but it's the way it is, the way I am. Maybe I pick hard women who can't share softness with me so I can be the soft one. Then I'll have something to complain about."

( *White Rage of Beauty* : 37 )

I hear rage or imagine it. I see Jeff as a nurturing breast with cold rage at its center, rage at women for not giving, for making him be the giving one. Only now no one is making him be anything. His makeup is making him be as he is. Is rage part of the coldness or the heat? Cold rage–hot rage? Being an amazing breast is not enough.

I see his mother, bony, held back, a straight line in the shadows. Does Jeff, the adored, know what his complaint is? What does a young mind make of the possibility that being adored nurtures the one who adores, that he feeds his mother through her idolization of him? And yet his radiance cannot cure her. She remains unfulfilled, in the background, parched and pinched. What trauma went into her contraction? So much hardship and injury compressed in his parents' backgrounds, he the flower from the soil. Yet he could not cure them. The food he gave his mother did not make her better.

Was he enraged at her because he was an impotent breast? All the idealization, glow, adoration — and when the smoke clears, she is still self-suppressed, bitter, quietly hurting, tucked away. If he was as wonderful as she made him out to be, then why did she keep sinking, fading? Did rage stop him from being sucked into the vanishing point? Where was the power of radiance to make radiant, to make self and other whole? And now he was enraged at his wife because his radiance couldn't cure *her*?

His practical wife with her depressive undertow. She was fuller than his mother, although trauma corroded her underpinnings. He picked people he could not cure and wondered if, after all, there was a secret logic to mystery and that he somehow failed to discern its outlines.

Most rage in life is quiet. Was there tacit agreement between mother and unborn child that adoration would substitute for rage, that there would not be room for a full range of feelings to flow between them? At times rage is sharp and crusty, but it can also be a thinning membrane, strung over years. Our capacity for feeling gets slanted by early filters and conditioning — human filters, the sensibility, responsiveness, and processing capacity of living beings. Is there always rage at self and others for not living up to idealizations?

And what of Jeff's specific problem? That an adored self was being foisted off on him in lieu of his mother's inability to be a fuller person, in lieu of traumatic stiffening? He reports seeing his mother out of the corner of his eye as more gaunt, hollow than she must have been and gets the idea she is a concentration camp survivor. He cannot grasp how he can be so cherished while she is starving to death.

Do we try to fix our parents and ourselves all our lives? That, of course, is not all, but isn't it part of our unconscious strivings? Rage at being broken, rage at the fixing process, rage at the inability to heal. Rage and grief feed each other.

Yet the core of love is genuine, and Jeff was loved. He glowed, he loved life. But love or self-love spread and blurred the details of how he, too, might be wasting away, raging away. His own starving self escaped notice. As soon as it threatened entry, self-idealization was pumped in to flood it. He could not bear awareness of deprivation very long: hence Paula on the horizon, someone better, more intact, someone he wouldn't have to cure, or so it seemed. Rose and Gwen started out that way too.

It's hard to grasp living two lives at once, two souls, nourishing and starving. Jeff couldn't assimilate (not yet) the coexistence of a nourishing and starving self. It was a blow to realize there were limits to what the nourishing-nourished sector could do, that digestion had difficulties and the flow of psychic blood passed aspects of self by. For the moment, it is enough to get transient intimations that his mother's starving face mirrors something in his child soul.

"I manipulated her into it. We were talking, she was telling me about being furious at work, how hard and awful it was for her. She's not been well. At work there are idiots and bullies. She was down. I don't know what made me do it. Did I plan to? Was it in my mind before she came? Have I been planning this for months? It just happened. I got aroused, and the more she talked the more aroused I got. I sat hoping it would pass. We were quiet awhile. I looked at her sympathetically. I saw her feel the rise of energy. Our eyes locked and I felt our bodies locking while we looked at each other, her face coloring. She had been so pale. Now when she spoke about her sense of injury, emotions were more available. Her rage at being taken advantage of shook her, and I could feel she was real. She was, too, furious at her own helplessness."

Fred was telling me about the fateful moment he lapsed into sexual contact with a client. He sought help because it was a condition the ethics committee of a professional group required if he was to continue practicing under its auspices.

"Could it be her helplessness aroused me? Or her rage?

"I can't say how honest I want to be here. I fear being too honest will get me into more trouble. I'm still being allowed to practice, but if I say too much who knows what will happen? I'm here because I have to be but want help too and know I have to be honest to get help."

"So we're in a bind here," I say. "I'm part of the police but supposed to be nonjudgmental so you can be yourself."

"I'm not sure what being myself is anymore. Being myself gets me in trouble. Maybe it's which self when. I'm a mess. Nothing's clear. It's hard for me to let myself be a patient. I'm not used to it. I'm used to being on the other side."

"Maybe you were trying to be a patient with your client, trying to get something from her. Maybe there's a way in which you've been a patient all along, disguised as a therapist." The words came out without thinking. I felt, in part, I was with a baby disguised as a man, trying to get mother to make him feel good.

"I heard her out and she felt some relief, and we were sitting with feelings getting stronger and I started rubbing my neck and acting as if I were in pain. She does massage and asked if she could help, and I hesitated but nodded. She felt for knots and traced them behind my shoulders, and after a while I sort of wriggled into position and took her hand and she knew what was happening and went down on me. We did this several weeks once a week. I stopped charging her, but we kept meeting because she felt I was helping her.

"She told her girlfriends what happened, and one of them was a therapist and reported me. She didn't want to stop seeing me and stayed nearly a year more before the whole thing blew. I had to stop seeing her, and she got another therapist. She felt badly about getting me in trouble but I got myself into trouble. She was talking about being taken advantage of, and I took advantage of her. She was talking about rage at bullies, and I sneakily bullied her. She talked about helplessness, and I played on compliance."

Fred went on about her good feelings blocking rage at him, he mirrored trauma that formed her, he was not fit to practice yet helped people. "Freud is right," he said. "We're at the mercy of drives, and ego finds ways to get what it wants. But not all therapists have sex with patients. This is not the way I usually behave. Something happened and I don't know what. I know about getting girls to do what you want—but not clients."

"Assuming we may never know for sure why this happened, let's keep exploring and see," I say.

"Her girlfriend expressed moral outrage for her," Fred continued. "She blew the whistle."

"Are you sorry?"

"Some ways yes, some no. You may think less of me, but I'm

not sorry for the pleasure, the warmth. I'm abhorrent, but not sorry for the closeness. It was a moment's gift, a reprieve from myself. Do child molesters feel this? The moment's warm pleasure was worth it. Also horrifying. I'm afraid for my skin, my profession. I hurt her. She felt helped by me and I blew her therapy out of the water. I wounded our work all the more because of the good in it.

"It's worse than you think. She does physical therapy in a clinic and makes extra money doing massage after work. She can't bear the way the clinic is run and what she has to go through to get patients the care they need. She found institutional work demoralizing. Then she'd go to men's apartments and do massage and sometimes bring them to climax because it happened that way, sometimes for extra money. I'd fantasize her doing it to me. One night I let down my guard, and in a few moments a good therapy relationship was over. As fast as an eyeblink, although it felt like slow motion.

"Could it happen again? I didn't know it *would* happen. I've practiced fifteen years and had sexual feelings with clients without anything happening. Now I *know* it *can* happen. But what do I know? That I don't know who I am or, worse, that I am who I feared I might be?"

"Like Oedipus, except with your patient, a secret mother? You keep saying client, a euphemism?"

"Mother baby sucking me, the strong one. Turning tables. Therapist as parent. You get a chance to be big. I picked up the term "client" in school, studying Carl Rogers. It stayed with me. I like it better than "patient." But I hear what you're saying. You're wondering if I protected myself from feeling how dependent and vulnerable people are when they need help.

"I violated vulnerability. I am a trauma. We are what we dread. I picture wounding and soothing a baby. I don't know who the baby is, my patient, myself? I feel the wound. Sucking soothes. Mother sucking. Baby sucking. I get a lot of crazy ideas about feeling big and weak. I see my patient as weak and big. She gets nourished sucking me. I'm her making myself feel better. I know I'm her. Except *her* therapy got ruined. I got her to make me feel big. But I feel the wound. There's no way out of this."

"First you have to get into it."

"I had a moral lapse."

"Maybe there's a realm of injury and pleasure where morality flies out the window."

"You don't mean morality isn't relevant?"

"No. I mean there's another focus."

"I do feel sorry, penitent. If I had it to do over, I wouldn't do it. I'll be better with other patients. I sound like an alcoholic saying I won't take another drink. I'm a person who can't be trusted, who can't trust himself. I have to live with knowing I'm that kind of person."

"Is it better to be that kind of person without knowing it?"

"You mean, something good can come of this? More self-knowledge?"

"Whether or not good comes remains to be seen. It's not a judgment I can make and seems besides the point to me right now. What's to the point is trying to feel what you feel and see what happens."

"It's feeling what I felt that got me into this."

"I don't think so. It's failing to that did. You didn't feel your feelings fully enough but stopped at a particular point. You enacted a particular scenario rather than stay with what might come up next."

"You mean I might not have done it if I had let myself feel the kinds of things coming up here? I would have been occupied with processes, not just my arousal? I lost the sense of sexual feelings having meaning. I wasn't even that aroused. A kind of fantasy arousal partly. I could have lived without it. What was I thinking? I didn't need this. What is wrong with me?

"I'm afraid of saying this, it shows how disgusting I am, but I see a Nazi throwing a baby in the air, bayoneting her, over and over. Something sadistic in me. Murdering a baby. But also me as a baby getting murdered. I'm a traumatized traumatizer. I traumatize a patient. Getting her to suck me is like bayoneting a baby. Traumatizing her therapy. Therapy is a baby. I'm a baby hater.

"What felt like a moment of weakness now seems an act of rage. It's crazy to say but what comes is I hate therapy. I want to destroy therapy. I destroyed hers. Her blowing me brings out something therapy is, an extended blow job. Maybe I was getting blown all along without knowing it. I only thought I was a therapist. And you? Are you a therapist? Is there any chance at all of me becoming a patient?"

Dependency and rage, weakness and rage, mixed with pleasure. Nursing. Or some kind of aborted nursing. Fred describes mixtures of megalomania, weakness, dependency, destruction, nourishment, soothing, caring, hating. He tried to stop the flow, or the flow became too much for him. He was overcome, gave in, and now must start the work again, dig deeper into the work. Pleasure became shock but may have muted shock to begin with. Is it sometimes necessary truly to shock oneself to move to another stage?

About a year into our work Fred got a letter from the client whose therapy he destroyed. She was in therapy with someone else and doing well. What happened with him so jolted her that after some of the shock waves lessened (she described going through rage and grief), she got a better job, stopped the massage work (which gave her a demeaning sense of power), and was trying to make something of herself. "I felt in a trance, going through life as if I couldn't do better,' she wrote. "What I did with you woke me up. I know you feel bad and think it was all your fault. But I think I needed something like that to make me realize I was someone. It was like staring into an abyss. My life flashed, and I saw myself going nowhere. While I was down on you my soul jumped out of me, lit up, smiled, said, 'Follow me.' It was like I was on my way to somewhere else. I guess I needed the whole thing to explode. I just wanted you to know I'm OK."

Fred wept and prayed he was on his way to becoming a better therapist, a better person.

# SHIT

A man given to wounding rages dreams shit drips from his ceiling. He wonders if something is wrong with his toilet, then realizes the toilet is outside, not inside his house. He is in a quandary as to whether to get a new one inside or hold on to the old outside one. A new one requires disruption, effort, investment. To make do with the old seems easier. He could drift along but starts to realize extra work now will make things better later. He really can't avoid seeing there is a problem with shit dripping, and the outside toilet does not do the trick. He may have to gather himself and face the fact that change is necessary. The dream shifts to classes and a teacher. Will he teach or go to class as a student?

Several days later he dreamt there were holes in the ceiling of his house needing repair.

"Well that's pretty clear," Frank admits. "Holes in my head. Shitty thoughts. Shit dripping, not pouring. That's improvement. At least I see there's a problem. Maybe it's not as bad as it was."

Frank was in therapy under court order, guilty of child and spousal abuse. He spent several months in jail and was given monitored and provisional visitation rights with his daughter when he got out. Caseworkers found him cooperative and hoped therapy and other forms of counseling and group work would help.

The judge let him off lightly. From long experience, she had a scale in her head weighing abuse committed with abuse potential, and Frank weighed in more salvageable than dangerous. The physical damage he had caused was superficial, and the enactments could be counted on one hand in eight years of family life. Nevertheless, he frightened his wife and daughter and shocked them with frequent rages. When the latter irrupted into something physical, his wife called the police and ended the marriage.

When I met Frank, I wondered if he had taken the judge in. He splattered intensely searching sincerity at me, and my guard went up. I feared being seduced by his will to cure. Rage does not let go its hold readily, and any chance of getting better is long and hard. I was glad he was in a group, a kind of "Ragers Anonymous," so there were separate checks in place to counter ability to fool himself.

"I'm not that bad," he said soon after we met. "I struck them but never beat them. I screamed, but that's not the same as beating the shit out of them." I was appalled by his lack of contact with himself and deficient sense of his effect on others. It was as if he said, "Hell, raging at people is not so bad. It only scares the shit out of them, makes them shrink, tiptoe, freeze, long for revenge." Frank showed a minimizing tendency bordering on denial.

In another breath he said, "I can't tell you how bad I feel. I was injuring my daughter, ruining my marriage, and couldn't help it. I'd give anything to do it over." When he said things like this, I could feel how doubled over he was inside, yet how futilely. "But I know I'd be pretty much the same," he confessed.

He felt bad yet shook it off—far from change one could count on. How *could* the court let him see his daughter? Perhaps because he was allowed to see her in controlled doses? He was appreciative. He did not want to lose these contacts. He also felt relief at having the visits monitored, a safety net protecting her from him, him from himself. With someone observing, he was afraid to be destructive. Fear helped. The court recognized a bond of love between father and child, albeit a love packed with rage and fear, the more intense for this fusion.

Everything I saw suggested Frank could fail. Wrenching sincerity oscillated with playing rages down, whitewashing them, brushing them off. "I must get better. I can't live like this." Yet he easily could live like this, all too easily. The pain of disability hadn't struck deep enough. The spike of who he was would have to be driven in more deeply before he pinned himself and stopped wriggling away.

He had the above dreams two years after I first saw him. Apparently the judge was right. In spite of fooling himself and pushing the results of his actions away, he hung in there, working as best he could.

A problem is that feeling sorry is not enough and can be a danger signal. One feels sorry for destructiveness, then the sorrow ebbs and the destructiveness builds, akin to an addictive cycle. I don't know what makes this tick, but both sides of the cycle go together, reparation-destructiveness. One is tied to both, needs both, wallows in both. In such a cycle, feeling sorry signals bad things to come.

There are people so identified with assertive impulses that for them reparation plays an unimportant role. They bully past fear and guilt, refusing to get bogged down by doubt or self-accusation. They are complemented by those so sensitive to signs of destructiveness, they are ready to hold back and apologize before they have cause to. Thus there are people who ought to be more afraid of themselves, as well as those who need to be less so. Most of us combine these tendencies, needing to be both more and less afraid of ourselves in different ways.

My initial impression was that Frank wasn't afraid of himself enough, he pushed fear of self away. Feeling sorry did not have the power to undercut remaining impervious to how jolting he could be. Maybe he found secret satisfaction in the impact rage could have.

In retrospect, I dismissed him as he dismissed his impact on those who were vulnerable to him. I was refusing to be vulnerable to him, impervious to his need for help. I felt he was trying to fool me, fool the system, fool himself. Now I believe the judge saw that too, but went beyond it. She sided with his good-hearted aspect, had faith in him, took a calculated risk to give him some kind of chance, at the same time providing guards to minimize damage if he failed.

( *Shit* : 47 )

There is overlap between therapy, prayer, and meditation, converging in a kind of faith, not knowing, openness. They coalesce in giving oneself another chance. The judge was ahead of me, but little by little I was catching on. There are moments when justice connects with principles of therapy-meditation-prayer and the heart has a chance to struggle with itself, even to open.

After two years of struggling with fear of opening, Frank was catching glimpses of himself. He could look at his dreams and begin to feel:

1. There are holes in his psyche.
2. He tries to plug the holes with shit.
3. The shit is his rage.
4. The shit represents the shitty things he does, the shitty life he lives, the shitty things done to him.

The dream is clear that what might deal with the shit is missing or in the wrong place, outside the self. The dream challenges Frank to build what is needed, to move from outside to inside himself, to have something inside to deal with psychic sewage. His psyche oozes shit and must find its way to the possibility of nourishment.

Holes in self begin to be felt. A sense of real weakness, deficiency, and disability is glimpsed in contrast with bravado, sentimentality, and self-pity fused with rage. Frank is hesitant to put in the work required to set things right. He fears some kind of loss—it feels like too much money and effort to install a working inside toilet. Yet incipient struggle is underway.

The stakes are compounded by Frank feeling his daughter as nourishment, the true gold of life. Perhaps letting in how his rage injured her was the most compelling spur to change. Love is real; she proves it. Love more real than shit. But shit ruins love, corrupts the gold. Damage is real. Love is real. Damaged love is real.

Therapy is a place to feel fleeting states more fully. Instead of feeling sorry and moving on to the next thing without being transformed, therapy slows things, so Frank rubs his nose in what is bad and keeps on rubbing. Session after session, week after week, month after month, he speaks about damaged states, rage wrecking the golden soul of a daughter, rage wrecking love. He must see over and over, taste in his pores shit splattering gold. He cannot escape it: rage ruins what he most loves. Therapy gives him time and a chance to feel the realness of damage. It is true and he must face it: Frank *is* disaster, yet not only disaster.

Dreams are bigger than what they image. They point to problems but also to possibilities of change. Here something outside ought to be inside, and, to some extent, Frank feels inside is growing. Near the time of these dreams, he said, "I was about to scream at kids in class when I choked it off. It stopped in my chest. It wouldn't move up through. I was amazed. I've stopped screams but not like this. This one stopped with a message. It stopped from inside the scream itself."

Frank taught school. For years he screamed at kids and felt justified because of their behavior. He wasn't the only one doing this. It seemed part of his profession, although, as he spoke more, he admitted feeling funny about it. "It really isn't right, but teachers do it, almost take it for granted, to get kids to behave. When they finally rile you to the breaking point, things quiet down." It's as if teaching, as he practices it, provides an outlet for rage. Now, Frank's conflict with rage was growing and rage stuck in his throat.

"I knew from an early age I existed to make my mother happy, to cater to her narcissism. I suppose I could have been a lot worse if the facts of life weren't so clear. Her ego was the center of our home. It was like a categorical imperative, the first commandment. In one way or another, we all distributed ourselves around that fact."

Thus George declared one day when he was speaking about difficulties with his wife. It began to dawn on him that he married someone who expected life to be centered around her ego.

"I didn't know any better when I was younger. I probably don't know any better now. And I'm not sure what good it does to start to know such things. I feel powerless in the face of my life. Things happen—you make what you can of them."

He paused. I could hear his breathing. He struggled with tears.

"I'm enraged at my life. I'm enraged at life itself, that it should have put me in such a position, that it could expect me to surmount it. I think life takes pleasure in smashing itself. Avalanches, explosions, death—yes, life certainly self-destructs as part of the whole system. Why shouldn't it work that way in my life too, in its infrastructure, in my pores?"

He is quiet a long time. His breathing is still audible but has subsided into a slow, steady rhythm. The tears are gone. He is no longer choking on himself. Then a sudden crescendo.

"I am absolutely enraged at my compliance. A good boy. I am a good boy. I can't stand it and can't stop it. I will be enraged at myself the rest of my life.

"I think my wife married me because I was a good boy who would be a good husband. And I am a good husband, a devoted father. I don't think I would break up my family. I don't know how bad it would have to get for that to happen. It's pretty bad now. I don't want to leave my kids: I can't. It would rip my heart out. I'm not going to be *that* bad to myself. But am I being worse by staying? Am I really ready to give up my life to be with my kids? My kids are my life. Anyway, what life do I have to give up? Whichever way I look, it's ugly, but there are moments of beauty with my kids."

Life goes on on many fronts at once. George feels his wife, Janice, replicates his mother but also knows and feels that this isn't so or isn't the only truth. For one thing, he and Janice fight all the time, everything from bickering and chronic irritability to screaming fits. They are scared for their children, who must be traumatized by this. But they cannot help it. He is fighting for his life. A lot of his compliance is imaginary. In fact, he incessantly fights against his situation. They fight to save themselves from going under, from losing self or position, to avoid being dethroned and rendered subservient.

Imaginary compliance can be lethal. It never lets up. Any intimate interaction may veer toward a territorial threat. Afraid of giving in and being no one, one fights for a place against a sensed power. There is always real enough justification, since one's partner, too, is trying to stay alive, further his or her life, and that can mean trouble—one is always in danger of losing out.

George is almost always in a state of rage or ready to be. This stops him from doing the work he wants to do. Instead of getting to it, he wiles hours playing video games, partly as an attempt to soothe himself and feel a bit of peace. He spends hours soothing rage away and dampening the sense of being compliant. George keeps attacking himself for being compliant, as if this were the whole truth about himself, a zealous and painful judgment.

As our work goes on, I share with him the following impressions, here condensed. "You defend yourself against your wife's demands and lack of recognition by readiness to attack. In fact you are justified or feel justified since she attacks or ignores you. You never get the sense that you and she respect each other. She is ever

ready to tear you down or feel you do not exist. You are always doing the wrong thing and so is she. You end up attacking both her
and yourself because you cannot feel your anger does any good.
You cannot feel that it gets through to her. It's as if you try to get
through to yourself and fail at that too."

"I keep wounding myself because I can't wound her to my satisfaction. But that is not all of it. It's as if I keep sticking my rage
into me to get all sorts of wounds to fester, all the injuries in my
life congealed—I go after them with my rage. I open myself by
opening my wounds. I won't let them heal."

"Because they heal the wrong way?" I ask.

"Yes, because I am marred by the healing process. The healing
is like scar tissue that twists me out of shape."

"You're hoping something different will happen here, that another kind of healing is necessary—possible?"

"That's what we're testing out—is it possible? Must I accept the
twistedness?"

George is enraged at the twistedness. He can accept the fact that
there is warp in life. "After all," he once opined, "Isn't space warped?
And so everything in it—including me, my self, my feelings? And
Janice? And you? Could my parents be anything but warped?

"But there is warp and there is warp. Not all warps are the same.
Maybe there is something I can do with all this that I haven't been
able to yet."

I agree with George, feeling there is more that can be done. At
the same time, I feel my warp, my twist. Congealed hate and fear,
trauma corpses that never let go, a sickly tail one drags through the
center of one's being. What have I done with it? Has it lessened
over the years or come to take less space? It keeps burrowing like
a spore deeper into healthy tissue, into depths one didn't know existed. Yet I feel something has happened and keeps happening.
Something does make a difference.

Is it only a change of attitude toward the twist, a broadening or
opening of self? A discovery that *jouissance* runs through it, that experience is delicious? Love runs through it? Something more?

Still, does daily life have to be such hell? Can anything make it better for George and Janice?

More than once, George said something like the following: "I feel I'm trying to blow myself up with rage, blow a hole through me, blow the pain away, blow the wounds out of existence. But then I come back, re-form, and I feel the hardening again, the cement, and I want to blow it away again. I want to blow myself away and still be there, survive, without the rage, without the giving in, the compliance, without so much injury. Do I want to be just me, a regular me, or something impossible, a me without pain. No, I'm willing to undergo the normal pain of living, I think. I'm ready to participate, to be a partner. Am I kidding myself?"

I get the sense he and Janice are siblings fighting over imaginary goodies. Each imagines the other feeds him or her shit. Both feel they give more than they get, that there is something the other gets that leaves him or her deprived. Perhaps one thing that separates George's marriage from his childhood is the rage he lives out in the former. He does not just fit in. Janice is not just mother — she is also an object of sibling rivalry. Perhaps rivalry is part of most situations, challenging us to deal with competing demands. How do we manage to hear each other and survive? And if we don't find ways to hear each other and ourselves, what will survival be like?

"I guess it's a matter of chipping away. We keep chipping away at the congealed stuff, the rage, the compliance. We keep working with it and something keeps happening, no?" I say what I feel, my truth, my faith.

"Yes, something is happening," George agrees. "How can I say that, I don't know. Since I still have the same problems. I'm as up against it as ever, in some ways more. But something is happening, it's so. I do feel more of me, more of Janice, even if I can't stand it. I say the worst of it here, you know. There are a lot of good things happening for me now. I want more, I want it to be better. Still, it really *is* as bad as I say."

To what extent does therapy appeal to compliance and elicit

rage? Is a moment of shared resonance a threat to self that triggers rage, a self-destructive survival instinct? Does George give in to me by acknowledging something is happening, or is he going deeper than compliant rage in witnessing something generative working in us?

As I get to know George, I am touched by his feeling for his children. There is, I feel, something in his self-sacrificial side that saves him from himself. Because of hatred of compliance, he could become a self-assertive monster, refusing to go deeper. People carry self-sacrifice to monstrous extremes too. But so far, I believe, George is lucky to be able to feel so deeply for his children. It brings him to another level in life.

Still, George and Janice's feelings for their children make them angrier at each other, insofar as they compete for their children's love. There is unconscious fantasy of total possession—each parent vying to be the God of the first Commandment ("Thou shalt have no other gods before me . . . I am a jealous God"). Loving and rageful.

In this regard, family life is a kind of primal swamp, a seedbed of possibilities, a lot of ugly life in hidden places, seething existence. Destruction is compost. Trauma waters as it warps. Litters grow, sustain losses. Life teems in tangled ways.

Someday George may sense something precious preserved in the casing of compliance, if the latter is an offshoot of a larger tendency involved with sensing what another feels, surrender, giving of self. To open to the impact of another can be a thrilling and enlarging thing. Too often one uses a partial tendency to devalue a greater reality, taking a particular form of self for the whole.

———

George began to draw. In therapy, creative urges tend to surface, whether one is an artist or not. I liked George's drawings: they felt alive to me. But whether I liked them or not, I probably would have been happy that something more or different was coming into being.

In drawing George found moments outside family hell. It is wonderful that in art a whole range of feelings can be expressed in a few strokes, often without realizing it. Not only old feelings. In art the present presses, something new seeks being. Reality creates itself as it goes along, with new twists, intimations, apperceptions.

For a time, George did not finish his drawings, and it felt good to let them remain incomplete, wanting more. It felt good not to have to finish, tie things down. "I get the sense they're trying to leave room for something." This went along with opening space for experiencing, space for self.

"When I was younger I tried to draw. I started things and stopped, scattered things about. I never was serious about it. I don't know if I'll stay with it now. I mean, I don't plan to make a living with it. But it might have graced my life. It was something I might have loved, at least enjoyed. I think I didn't keep it up, if you can imagine, because it felt too good. I couldn't take how good it felt. There is a secret ecstasy in drawing. An ecstasy in lines, forms, color. Just to feel your hand moving across a pad, lines spurting, curving, crisscrossing before your eyes, seeing changes you couldn't imagine seconds before. Where does it come from? How does it happen? It's like having your own little orgasm inside you. You light up as soon as you touch a pencil. A blank page seems so alive—you can feel what may grow in it without knowing what."

We were peacefully quiet for a while, like lovers after sex.

"You know, maybe it's too good for me here. Therapy can be misleading. It's not like life. I don't get as hurt or mad here as I do with Janice or as frustrated as I do with my kids. Maybe something's wrong with my therapy. Why don't I get mad at you more? You give me space to go wherever I go. Maybe I'm just a good boy here like everywhere else, afraid to give you too tough a time."

"You're afraid that the good space in therapy is making you angrier at home?"

"Yes. Maybe if I were angrier here, I'd be easier at home."

George is right. The time will come when therapy rage has its day. For the moment, I'm too nice, making things too easy, not at all demanding and accusing like his wife. This makes things harder for his wife. She looks still worse, compared to me. George is experiencing secret pleasures in therapy, a little womb or space for hidden psychic orgasms. The warts on the witch's nose of real life can't compete with therapy ecstasy. Some of the latter spilled over into his art.

There were, also, moments of good sex with Janice. When they were younger, this was the rule, not the exception. As their family grew, battles increased and their sexual life suffered. The struggle for survival, power, or control took its toll. Sex gets worn down by hostility. Now hints of sex surfaced again, beaten down quickly by bickering and picking on each other. At first, it was not that Janice looked better to him (or he to her). It was probably more a rise of feeling in general. As ecstasy arose in art and therapy, even if in hidden ways, sexual feeling pushed through with it, part of the tide.

Then, one day, George came in shocked. "My secret ecstasy is spreading. I felt it for Janice. It came over me in an instant. I was walking down the street, taking a break from work. A sunny, breezy day—I was feeling good. Then I saw Janice in my mind, my mind's heart, aglow, beautiful. I felt love—for her, yes—but just love—love. It sounds awful to say, but she's the last one I'd expect to love. We've become enemies. We're at war. I'm not sure I want to love Janice, not be in love with her. That would be way too dangerous. I'd get killed. She couldn't handle it. I'd be afraid.

"I mean, I guess it would be great if I could feel that with an-other person, but it does not seem possible. I don't know if that will happen for me, not with Janice. I'd have to find someone out-side our marriage, and I'm not sure I'll ever be able to do that. It's not a risk I want to take. Then it shifted all inside me. I felt love in my heart for a Janice I might never know. I felt I knew her essence and her essence spread through me. It was the Janice I thought I fell in love with years ago. An image in my soul that might or might not have too much to do with the real person she is today. Maybe I do not want to know the actual Janice because she does not fit the Janice in my heart."

"The heaven within."

"Yes, but what do I do with it? I feel it, and it makes me feel good. But it gets me in trouble in real life. But I would not want to be without it. It's the greatest thing that's happened to me since having children. It's one of the greatest discoveries of my life."

The bickering and infighting went on. "It's more like background noise. I don't pay as much attention to it. It's a distraction. I try to focus more on my drawing and how I feel then. The thrill inside that makes Janice seem heavenly for a time. It's a life-feeling in me I knew I had but couldn't access much before. I'm more interested in what it feels like to be me than in the stupid fights we have."

Hell continues. "I forget for a while how bad it is because I feel better. Then something happens and I'm brought up short and the contrast is more than I can bear. The anger never stops. We can't let go and cut each other slack. Will it ever get better?"

The rage to live is a powerful force. But what happens when it turns against itself?

Individuals feel persecuted by the urge to exist. The force to exist may press a woman to have babies she does not want or that her personality cannot support, birthing situations like bombs damaging personal life.

In describing a woman in such a situation, Bion writes, "And this urge is completely indifferent to human beings; it doesn't care whether we die in childbirth or in any other way. Her parents' urge to exist forced them to give birth to a child whether they wanted one or not. So she herself is the product of the same urge and is at its mercy. She is frightened of being all alone with that urge to exist which doesn't mind what happens to her—it is completely ruthless."

We are inhabited by something ruthless. At times, we identify with it but also may draw back in horror at the possibility of being taken over by forces we do not control. We draw back in horror, discovering that this possibility may, indeed, be the rule. We blindly strike out at processes that create and sustain us but that also can be too much for us. It is difficult to feel at a loss and confess our partnership with ourselves is experimental.

"I" or personal being spreads through body and consciousness and unconsciousness, fusing with and putting a stamp on anonymous, impersonal being. *I* think, *I* feel, *I* believe, *I* dance, *I* talk, *I* pray, *I* play. The cozy I'ing of our bodies and minds can be brought up short by catastrophe or acute inner awakening to the seas of being we float on and are pummeled by. The I itself can be felt to be anonymous, since we all share it, and in our I-ness are, in some sense, clones of one another.

I fighting I in public ↔ I fighting I in private.

I sprinkles identifications throughout mental-physical functions. Math people, poetry people, sports people, psychoanalytic people, people people. Myriad permutations. It may be some part of me grew in a special way because I identified with it, or it may be I identified with it because it grew. Then again, a person may be at war with his talents and feel persecuted by the demands of something growing in him. Otto Rank depicts conflict between the drive for artistic identity and the need for personal life, the former feeding off, disregarding, even destroying the latter (the reverse also possible).

Jacques Lacan implies that drives are split and thoughts and feelings contain their own antithesis, even their own self-nulling. Bion adds, "For something to exist, it must both be and not be at the same time." This applies to I. Our I possesses the amazing capacity to null itself and would not be the sort of I it is without this capacity. +I and −I occupy the same space, *are* the same space.

It is possible for a person to be persecuted by his own I. This is probably the rule rather than the exception. It is a difficult fact to take in because being an I gives one so much pleasure. How can something that is so pleasurable be so painful? Stakes are multiplied as I approaches infinity: infinite pleasure, infinite pain. Pleasure and pain give way to ecstasies and agonies. Emotional infinities−I infinities fuse.

One persecutory scenario: +I and −I persecute each other, a little like a diseased rat eating its own limb. Either side of I can be shortsighted and not encompass the other. Aspects of I-infinity war against other aspects. +I is persecuted by −I and vice versa, an eternal struggle waxing and waning. If I fails to recognize its own division, or +I/−I wishes more unity than possibility allows, frustration may lead to more splitting and intensify attempts at fusion.

Optimally, +I/−I friction leads to further development. Inevitable +I/−I tensions lead to development in less than optimal conditions too (which is what usually happens). Development is always partly frozen, partial, stifled or deformed. The I's attempt to make things better often makes things worse, partly owing to incomplete views of what it tries to heal and how. Failing to work with oneself makes things worse too. Intermittent attempts to work with oneself at least keeps open the possibility of learning something more about one's situation.

Rage to live and rage against life are part of life's doing-undoing itself. Life can recoil against itself at almost any level. Life against life. With us it reaches new proportions, insofar as sensitivity is infinitized. A person can feel persecuted by sensations, emotions, thoughts. There are people for whom light or sound or touch can be excruciating. I've heard artists speak about being painfully flooded by light and colors, unable to bear sensitivity to impact. On the other side of the spectrum (not unrelated) are individuals who nearly pass out from the ecstatic impact of beauty.

Recoil against impact can refer to inner or outer stimuli of many sorts. Psychesoma can attack or try to null its capacity to sense, think, or feel, including kinesthetic and proprioceptive sensation. It may attack or recoil from respiration, digestion, neural transmission, even, finally, disrupt the immune system's capacity to do its work. Self-nulling may be driven to quite some extreme before finding satisfactory zero points.

Blind rage and resistance against zero can quicken the rage for zero.

The capacity to experience may turn against itself as a matter of course to help modulate input and flow. Inhibition and suppression are part of selection and attention. Shutting off and opening up can work together. We endure intensity, then need recovery time. Lowering and raising the volume of experiencing is part of learning to work with ourselves.

There may be mid-ranges of experiencing most people tolerate well enough. Even this is premised on a lot of shutting out, ignoring vast terrains of experience and devaluing (or idealizing) what is dismissed. Too often some mid-range sector is proposed as normative, depleting creative possibilities of the larger whole. This is one way sensitivity turns against itself, fearing idiosyncratic excess.

Sensitivity's rage against itself can be total and gruesome, attempting to undo the possibility of any sensitivity at all. Suicide and murder are related extremes in which sensitivity seeks to blot out impingements—basically its own sensitivity, the vulnerability of aliveness. But there are many lesser ways individuals tear at sensitivity, irritating it to the point of numbness, then tearing at it some more. On the other hand, sensitivity, also, grows more finely attuned, shutting out or ejecting what it must in order to let areas of interest grow. It is not unusual for something set aside at one phase to become essential at another or for a new sense of what is possible to emerge.

Rage of sensitivity against itself, inability to bear itself, including reservoirs of self-hatred, seeps into subsystems of personality, poisoning portions of life, seeping deep into body, sometimes draining body of life itself. We are in nursery school learning what we can about maximizing benefits of being sensitive beings while minimizing sensitivity's destructiveness.

"The head of my penis falls off in my hand," says Warren. "Karen rejected me. She didn't return my calls. This happens a lot. I call people, want to see them. They don't call back. I call again and they make excuses."

It is not the first time Warren has dreamt of body part loss, nor the first time his penis or part of it has fallen off. It might be the first time he caught it. I remember an earlier dream in which his penis fell into a toilet. "Is this the first time it fell into your hand?" I ask.

"It's quite an extreme hand job," he continues. "I used to be afraid it would come off as punishment for masturbation. Now I picture playing catch with it. I imagine my son's baseball team playing catch with penis heads. It's a deep fear. I can remember being afraid of my penis coming off ever since I was a little boy. I used to lay in bed watching it get bigger and smaller, frightened it would drop off. Once, in a panic I asked my mother to come and watch it. I was afraid it was coming off, and she told me that's the way penises are, it wasn't coming off. I had a sense I got her worried for a minute. I'm so grateful I've never had sex with my children. I was always afraid of that. Maybe I think I can't have sex with them if I don't have a penis.

"When I get rejected, fears like that come up. Since I get rejected often, or feel I do, I'm always feeling afraid. It scares me getting rejected can make my penis fall off. I guess it's good I caught it. There's some degree of containment. I'm not entirely splattering, falling apart, am I?"

I thought of saying, "You have to try to hold yourself together because you feel I won't be able to help you?" or some remark about having to do it himself because he can't rely on me. But I thought better of it and waited. I didn't want to inject myself too quickly and take his experience away from him.

"In Rosh Hashanah we have a fish head and pray to be the head rather than tail in the coming year. Is the penis a kind of tail, a funny tail on the other side? I feel like a tail and try to make believe I've got a head. My wife tells me not to lose my head. That was a thing in my family. When I was growing up everyone lost their heads. A frightened, worried family, always flying off in rages. I could see their heads blowing off. That was another phrase, blowing off steam. 'I'll kill you if you make another sound,' my father said repeatedly. He'd go crazy over little things. He and my mother lost their heads at the slightest excuse, the smallest provocation.

"I guess I can finally put my penis in my mouth, if I've got its head in my hand. I used to have dreams of blowing myself. I used to try to do it. I thought it would be great, but in my dreams it wasn't so great. It was a little weird. Like trying to plug a hole, fill a gap, make myself a complete circuit, intact, whole. I feel like crying. It's sad to be so pathetic, to need to soothe my crazy, worried rage."

Again the sense of Warren doing it himself, no one helps him. He has to find ways, often extreme ways, to hold himself together. At the same time I sensed he could not be talking like this if I were not in the background.

"So blowing myself is a way to stop blowing myself up. Everyone blew up in my house. Everyone was worried and blowing up. I grew up in panic and rage. That was the air I breathed.

"I blow myself to make sure I have a penis. I'm always afraid of losing it. I lose it anyway. I can't pretend I'm not an injured person. I can't make loss go away. I try to put myself together with my mouth, like putting myself together here with words. Nursing wounds.

"I'm fragile, fragmented. Rage puts me together. I rage at my wife and kids. Blow up over nothing. Anything can be an excuse. My wife and kids do things I don't like and I go crazy. I pick on weaknesses in their personalities. I can't stand my wife's hemming and hawing. She vacillates this way, that way. I think she's decided, then she says, well, maybe some other way. I blow up. She seems so hapless. She can't stand my excitement, although I know that's one thing that drew her to me. I show more feeling than she does.

"My kids are the same way. They say one thing, do another. I'm all over them. My wife tells me to lay back and cut them more slack. She says she won't put up with my rages anymore. But she's no innocent.

"I'm much better since therapy. I control myself more. Sometimes I feel it coming and nip it. I monitor myself a little better. My wife sees improvement but wants more. I know I have to keep working at it. I'm hurting the kids. I'm hurting my marriage. I'm only like this at home. I don't blow up at work or with friends. I think of myself as a good friend and a hard worker.

"Losing my head, my power, my pleasure. My truest joy is when things go well with my family and there are good, rich times. I love my work. I feel creative there. If I lose my creativity at home, things go badly. I have to get used to the idea that life at home is frustrating. People don't do what I want. They do their own thing. They don't do things the way I would, the way I want them to. Everyone goes their own way. I ought to be happy for them, to appreciate this. If I step back, I can take this in. I expect differences at work and deal with them. At home there's slippage. I expect to relax, let down, and imagine things will be easier. In a way, home is harder than work. It's hard to accept this. I let down, get caught up, and freak out. It's not just that I'm insecure sexually—although that's true enough—but I lose power, strength, mind. I fear losing my masculinity and blow. I fear losing my mind, my self, and blow—but that *is* losing my mind, isn't it?

"I'm stuck. If I step back, I lose. If I blow—I lose."

"Which way would you rather lose?" I ask.

"Do I have a choice? I never felt I had a choice. Coming and talking about this, something happens, a shift inside, maybe something to build on."

"How do you lose by stepping back?" I ask, returning to his previous remark.

"I feel like I'm giving in to the other person. I think they've won. I think they think they've won. If I don't beat them down, they get satisfaction, a victory. Also, I fear holding myself back will damage me."

"Like not shitting?" I ask.

"Yeah. A build up of poisons. I think it's not good for you to sit on your feelings, keep it all in. But exploding is a loss of self too. It cows the other person for a while, it doesn't really beat them. It used to feel more like a win to me. It's not as big a pleasure anymore. I've begun to hate myself for it, see it as weak, a sense of victory at my own expense."

Is holding back feelings really analogous to holding back waste material? Feelings, after all, are ineffable and lack material shape and tangibility. One can focus on feelings and experience transformation processes. There is an apparent analogy between holding back shit and feelings, but the divergent domains bring us to very different places. My sense is that Warren is on the brink of discovering how different feelings are from feces, but he tends to conflate them. He is, too, alert to the tug of power, who will win or lose at any moment. He cannot bear seeing the other's winning face in his mind—and has begun to be aware that there is a face inside he cannot stand. Quite a journey lies ahead. In the meanwhile, he voices helplessness in the face of vulnerability. He returns to being rejected by his friend, Karen.

"When I get rejected by Karen, I'm hurt and furious. I'm furious she doesn't call. I thought we were friends. Was it all in my mind? I try to think she's busy or something went wrong in her life. But the truth is she's too busy for me. She doesn't want to make the effort to be with me. The click comes. Pain and fury, outrage."

He's covered the vulnerability—rage as cement. Pain continues in the rage, fueling the latter. He rages to get rid of the pain, which continues as fuel. There is also the picture of Karen's face inside his mind, fusing with rejecting faces generally. He pictures the winner gloating.

"If I didn't have you to talk with, my life would be in shambles. I'd make a mess in no time. I'm messing up as it is. Coming here provides some damage control. I'm so vulnerable if someone doesn't look at me the right way. I fall apart, blow up. There's an explosion waiting to happen. Maybe it's always happening and just surfaces at certain times. An explosion going on and on. I think I'm like that. Coming here slows me down a little. I get a chance to let it out, think about it. It's hard to talk about it with my wife because we blow up at each other. Our fuses are short. Here I can talk. You don't stop me. You don't jump in and get angry and tell me how much I'm hurting you, how bad I am. You give rage room. In real life it breaks things, people, the ones I love the most. For a long time I feared it would break therapy. But therapy goes on and on."

"Like rage? You thought therapy would fall apart like your dream penis?" I ask.

"Who would put it together again, my Humpty Dumpty penis? I feel I'm the one who keeps things together. I'm the one who blows apart and has to make it better. My parents always made me say I'm sorry. I hated that. Endless apologies. Always doing something wrong and making up to them. They were crazy. My father took a lamp and banged it on the table, threatening to smash me with it. 'You see how it broke?' he said. 'You're bones will break.' Rages, menacing looks. I was terrified. I should apologize for him breaking lamps? No wonder I can't stop raging. It's too much work holding myself together. With the family I came from, what did I learn? You handle things by getting mad? I can't undo a lifetime."

"You have to keep therapy together too?" I ask.

"I feared showing you what I'm like. But I'd think, 'If he doesn't know, how can he help?' There's a line I'm afraid to go over. The line keeps changing but is still there. When I blow up at you, the rage falls into a quiet place. You wait, wait, wait. I hear you breathing. I'm convinced your breathing is a kind of thinking. I get the idea you want me to think through breathing."

"Now?"

"I don't know. Sometimes you tell me to breathe. You told me to breathe when I get mad at home, concentrate on my breathing when I'm upset, feel my breathing. You want me to think with my breathing too. Sometimes I do. Sometimes I feel a quiet place inside like I feel here. "

"In the rage you're puffed up and small?" I ask.

"Big and small at the same time," Warren continues. "My chest puffs, inflates. I feel bigger, engorged. Big while my penis is falling off! Falling apart, puffed up. I puff up and my breathing stops. My chest is puffed and deflated at the same time. That sounds impossible.

"Breathing holds me together, not only rage. That's something I'm learning here. Breathing between pain and rage."

The gloating face keeps rage going and vice versa. So much of the self is unformed, chaotic, porridgy, "neonic," liquid, diffuse. Rage provides a sense of power in the face of (1) the gloating face and (2) porridgy innards. It is self-defeating if personality fails to evolve with it or if it destroys possibilities of living. Rage, also, can evolve—there are more and less "mature" rages, although the baby self marks rage in every context. A baby screams in pain—and rage against injustice involves economic, social, psychological, ethical, spiritual pain.

On the other hand, self tightens, hardens, becomes stuck in terror/rage. Tightness runs through will and body. Warren sees and hears his father breaking lamps and bones in his mind's eye. Psychic presences are saying, "I'll split your head," and this saying is also a doing. Warren is ever being split and broken, porridgy and tight. Almost any threat triggers a sense of other threats, mushrooming backward and forward through his life. Waves of threats unite multiplicatively. Threat-pain-rage fuse and magnify, spread through his body—*become* his body. In Warren's case, fear-rage was a prominent part of the world he was born into, part of what he learned, what his body absorbed. In his family, rage was part of love. At moments, rage *is* love and hunger for love.

I agree with Warren: one can't undo a lifetime's learning. Still, as Warren hints, therapy can provide breathing time, time to feel what one is stuck in, feel it some more, and, slowly, other feelings start to grow. Rage cannot be tempered without broadening the range of what one can imagine. The gloating face (perversely infuriating, mesmerizingly transcendental), the lamp smasher (fusional-explosive body) seep deep into one's being, become funnels for being. Somehow listening to my breathing Warren tunes into another kind of thinking, and it becomes nearly impossible to stop imagining different possibilities of otherness, different nuances of self, whetting the appetite of a hunger that frees.

Warren weeps a long time. Another kind of flood, tears that never stop, watering the soul. "I'm so injured. Terribly injured," he sobs.

"You once told me I am pain," he continues. "I'm not pain. I'm in pain. I hate because I've been hurt, annihilated, wiped out, threatened. Past figures loom larger than life in my mind. Areas of my being are wiped out. My hate fills wiped-out areas. It means to stop destruction but destroys more. I'm still at the level of trauma. They [his parents] still cause me pain. I picture myself trying to play with them as a child. It was playing with calamity."

The sobbing becomes angrier.

"My anger is right. It stops me from falling forever," he says.

"Falling forever is a moment," I say. "It's not the only moment."

"I know you're telling me I need to disintegrate, feel the anxiety, come back together naturally. Like breaking a bone over and over until it heals right. I feel my balls but not my penis. It's scary not to feel my penis. It happens to me out of the blue. I become aware I'm not feeling it. It's blank there. I can't feel it from the inside. It's part of falling forever. The head of my penis would fall forever if I didn't catch it. I lucked out in the dream. I might have lost myself forever."

"Because you don't feel it right now doesn't mean it's not

there," I say. Because something's absent doesn't mean it doesn't exist.

"What would it be like without hate?" Warren muses. "Without hate, I wouldn't be someone to be reckoned with. I would be less special. I couldn't ward off helplessness. Hate connects me to some kind of special identity. My passion is hatred."

Warren sobs, sobs more fully than ever.

**M**organ speaks of being a connoisseur of pain and anxiety. His sensitivity magnifies small shifts of being that he is forced to attend to. He has been this way for as long as he can remember and is still not used to it, although he has learned a lot about how to be the kind of person he is. A sensitive magnifier has advantages too, if one views attunement to injury as important.

One of the things that most bothers Morgan is that he is a rageful person. He is filled with rage that does not go away, never-ending rage. He has learned the hard way to control it. But like an alcoholic, he knows he can give in any time, that it can possess him and scar those around him.

He was born to a family of ragers and knew at an early age that he was split. On the one hand, he was frightened, inhibited, stunted. On the other, he was impulsive, capable of lashing out any time. Impacted and explosive. He remembers vowing to himself, perhaps at eight years old, that he would not be cowed by his nature—he must find ways to make the most of his life. It was a vow he renewed frequently.

Now in his mid-fifties, he has become a delicate, exquisite person, a successful consultant who mediates disputes for businesses. Sensitivity to injury helps him take in multiple viewpoints and develop alternate strategies for working together. He is, too, raising a family and knows too well how inadvertent outbursts burn holes in a child's soul.

He is furious that he is still furious, that he has to be vigilant at all times and can never let down. He has become a self-watcher on permanent guard duty. One day at a time, a minute at a time, moment to moment. "A river of rage runs through it," he says about life, a remark similar to those I've heard from many ragers angry at having to scare themselves so.

"You don't judge me. You don't say, 'You're not letting yourself feel the good things.' That's an insidious judgment our culture makes." Morgan reflects for a moment, then continues, "This idea that it's up to you to feel good—it's an awful pressure. The idea that I feel bad because I make myself feel bad, that I get in the way of my feeling better—what a crushing idea. It's judgmental. It's really saying, 'You're bad for feeling bad. If you were good, you'd feel good.'

"I don't want to be a rageful person. I didn't make myself this way. I'd give anything to be different. I've tried everything. I've had to learn to make the best of it, rage underneath—always. I understand the ethics of it and meet the struggle with myself. But it doesn't go away. I don't go away.

"One thing that makes it possible to keep coming here is you don't tell me it should be different, no false hope. You hear me out, know my suffering. I sense you think there's more, but not the same more society pushes. I don't believe you're trying to sell me anything; it's something else.

"You're not telling me the pain and damage is buried in the past, something to get past, that now is now and I can be different. You know the pain and damage is real right now, alive, raw, hellish, the most alive thing I know. Wishing it were different doesn't change it. It outlasts everything. I am damaged, and the damage is painful. It doesn't stop—damage goes on damaging. I think a lot of people feel this but won't let themselves know. There's nothing to be done, so why know? It's there, eating away at people, society—look at what's out there! Look what we do to ourselves and each other!

"We had a lot of lovemaking on vacation and walking early morning in the woods. I could let some of it in, feel beauty more, not simply appreciate it abstractly as usual. Pain and terror ready to shut it down, on the verge of shutting down, always feeling the shutdown happening. A year ago I couldn't let this much in. I

( *Underneath* : 71 )

didn't think this much possible for me. Infinitesimal to someone else—unbelievable for me. The shutdown is there waiting. It lets up maybe as long as an eyeblink.

"Our children tell us how difficult it is living with us. A tremendous struggle for us all. Barrie thinks she can lord it over us we're so bad. She sees I'm bleeding and uses that as an excuse to get away with murder. This must be some kind of experiment in family living, all out in the open. Melissa [Morgan's wife] and I found ourselves taking up a position, insisting whatever is wrong with us, we all require respect. They came around a little."

Lovemaking, walking, struggling with children to put family on workable ground. Morgan fills me in after his vacation—the battle to support core respect for everyone in the cauldron of the family. How can his children not be in for rough times? Yet they were fighting for something good at the heart of it. They reached points where they stood up for and to each other.

Morgan dropped to another plane, deep in his own beginnings. "Loss happened too early, so I couldn't prepare for loss later in life." His mother and father hated each other, and Morgan was ripped from one to the other. Each took him for periods, and when he was with one, he lost the other. It seemed he lost one or another parent from the time of birth. Some part of him was always being ripped away. "I didn't have a chance to get used to being. Loss is never normal for me. As I'm being born I'm losing a parent. In birth I lost myself. This rip is all of life. My mother was beautiful but dead. Not dead always, but when I needed her. She was dead to herself much of the time. She did not survive life well. Maybe I'm saying she did not survive me well. I've a terror of deadness in people's faces. I fear that in you, your dead spots, dead looks. Maybe you're not alive enough for me or, worse, you're pretending to be alive. I'm terrified of people living from dead places.

"I'm terrified of deadness in lovemaking, although I should be used to it by now. Lovemaking was good on vacation, deadness minimal—that makes it all the more scary. I have a gift for attunement—if attunement wasn't taken over by rage, hunger, desperation for revenge filling my body. The bad stuff is always rising or about to rise. Attunement triggers rage, rage is damaging, damage is painful, attunement is painful, beauty is painful. "Was Jesus really different? Was he one of those driven to be a philosopher king or a humble person, seeing injury, unable to bear it? Is it possible to be a prophet from a humble place, seeing and feeling the pain? Are there genuine leaders? Gandhi? Mandela? Good, benevolent leaders—is it possible? Or is it that power corrupts and that's that?

"Deflation follows worship. That's one reason I'm afraid to act, to go as far as I can. There is a thrust in me toward leadership, a difference between you and me. I have more facility than you in public—so I think. You're more awkward. I can extemporaneously carry a group along with me and people would follow, but I know my statements are only in a very superficial way true. I say things for effect and despise those who are taken in, who listen and believe, inferior all."

Yes, and what about therapy? Has it been for effect? Has Morgan let down, opened up, spoken truth? Am I the inferior believer to his mock Jesus? Can all his soul baring be a caricature? That is precisely what terrifies him. And my awkwardness—a caricature too? Morgan is right—there is no way out of this terror: not through pain or awkwardness, certainly not through truth. Rage breaks through momentarily to fall back behind bars, a trapped animal. It is part of pain and pain returns. Neither terror nor rage are for nothing, I feel strongly. Morgan feels the wheel spinning in his gut, cutting deeper, and wonders what I can know.

"hy do I come to see you? I don't know. A place outside the storm? My life is good. Most of the time we do nothing. I guess there's something to be said for doing nothing. I'm happy with my life. What is there to say? If my life gets any better, I'll burst. My writing's getting reviewed. I have plenty of girlfriends, more than I can handle. Is that a problem?

"Some people might think it's a problem, but—wow—it's what I always wanted, and now it's happening. I met three girls running in the past two days. I get the feeling I can meet as many as I like, the water is filled with beauty—throw the line in, another mermaid.

"I like each one when we're together. Then I see another and like her too. So many girls that are striking or good looking in one way or another. Each one feels good. Why is that a problem? It's not. You think I'm shallow, don't you? Well—I'm lucky."

I run around the park too and feel the jolt of women and imagine being with them. Camby actually does it. Who wouldn't envy him? Do I think he's shallow? Where did that thought come from? A fly in paradise? Do I put him down out of envy? I thought I was just listening. Is he picking up a flaw, and, if so, where is it located? In him or me or both of us? Why this uncertainty? He asked and answered the first question. Should I doubt he's lucky?

There was a time I doubted everything, tore self to pieces. It was a bloody business, trying to find something real, what personality is made of, what I'm made of, like the Greeks looking for first elements. Mind can blow up elements, go too far, dissolve everything to nothing. Then there are nothings to explore. Sweet nothings. Malevolent nothings. But I'm jumping way ahead of Camby. Perhaps he *is* lucky and won't have to find out what *he's* made of, miss the manure. Then why is he here? To celebrate himself? Who is made of what? "Every soul is a different species." In the struggle to be open, there is a great undertow.

"Where does your idea of shallowness come from?" I ask.

There is a pause. Camby had been going on happily. Should I have contained my doubt instead of spilling, my kind of mental promiscuity? Promiscuity—a judgmental term? Am I judging him, mirroring his actions with my mind? Doubting myself as usual? Didn't *he* say *I* thought him shallow? Who doubts who?

"I thought you thought that," he says.

"Well, the idea of shallowness appeared. But we don't know in whose mind. It almost sounds as if you said I think you're lucky to be shallow."

"It's just a way of speaking," Camby answers. I've made him defensive? He's made me defensive? We've become defensive together? "It's what society thinks. I must be shallow if I'm going around having sex with lots of women."

"Society is deep?" I muse.

He laughs.

"I feel we are being pressured by an idea of superficiality," I add. "Perhaps you feel our time is shallow, we are going nowhere. While you were wondering why you were here, a notion of shallowness appeared. You seemed to defend yourself against attack from an unknown origin."

"You're making too much of it," Camby replies. "It was just a thought."

"Yes, but whose thought? What may it mean?" Was I being silly, trying to hook a fish that was already on the table? "*Shallow.* What shall we do with it? Let the thought swim away, disappear in the mind?" Back to the flow, let it all come and go.

But a break had been made, a change from *I* to *you*—*you* must think, then a criticism. He was proposing to read my mind. Was he, indeed, doing it? And now, in turn, I was trying to read his? Or was I just asking a question, trying to slow things down?

After a time, Camby regroups. "It does sound like some kind of attack, doesn't it? It does sound like I'm calling myself superficial, attacking myself for getting pleasure, for having a good life, for doing what I want."

We sit with it.

"You've opened a can of worms, not letting me get away. I see it, and it's an old thing. My parents put themselves down. I used to think, 'I'm not going to be like them. I refuse to. I'm going to be free.' I pretty well succeeded."

Camby says more about his parents. They were hard-working people, dedicated to doing their best, but very self-critical. They were hard on themselves for not doing better. They reached a ceiling in life pretty early.

His father was an engineer who worked for the same company his entire adult life, rising in small steps, never breaking through to higher management. His reward was job security and a good reputation. Those above him could count on him. This he was proud of, but he felt like a failure for not getting further. Steady, reliable man—Camby felt suffocated by his father's sense of responsibility and sense of failure. As he thinks back to it, Camby says, "It drove me crazy. I flew into rages. He was so even-mannered. I can appreciate that now—but he seemed so controlled and stuffy then. I wanted to break out. 'What are you mad about?' they used to ask. 'There he goes again!' They tried kidding me out of it, but it was no kidding business. I used to scare myself flying out of control. It came out of the blue for no reason. I couldn't stop it. No one could. A menace. Very sudden, a seizure. It began going away when I was a teen, a little before, I think. I became sullen."

Camby's mother failed in several businesses. Unlike his father, she was her own boss and achieved modest success with a dress store. In the end, competition became too much and she had to close. She gave it a good run before throwing in the towel. Camby grew up in a house filled with complaints as she battled. She didn't lose herself in rages like Camby but was angry at the world of cut-throat competitors. She was always in danger of being edged out. The world was not big enough for everyone.

With his mother, Camby, too, felt edged out, pushed aside, not significant enough. He felt she didn't have enough time for him (and his two brothers). He could not compete with her business interests, although she gave what she could. He tended to be sullen with her, partly giving up on capturing more interest. Where he felt suffocated by his father's steadiness, he felt at sea with his mother's preoccupations. He was learning home was a place to get away from, a place he didn't want to be.

Camby barely got through college. "I didn't know what was happening most of the time. Swirls of beer parties, drugs, girls, most of whom I couldn't have. I was too shy. A desert in a flood. It was overwhelming. When I managed to reach out, I was awkward. I couldn't get in sync with anything or myself. It went by too fast, and I was in slow motion, shut off inside. I felt out of it in classes. What *were* they talking about? I didn't have a clue. How did I get through it?

"There were flickers of interest. I fancied being a writer but when I took a writing class, I thought, 'this isn't for me.' The teacher wasn't interested in me. I didn't know what anyone was talking about most of the time. Or if I knew, it didn't matter. Nothing stuck inside. I just didn't get it."

Rageful as a child. Sullen as a teen. Overwhelmed, out of it, shut off as a college student. My mind gravitated toward states spread over years, strung together like beads. A progression?

School, like home, was a place to get away from. Camby's first jobs after college came and went—writing advertising copy, waiting on tables. He traveled some, wrote some. He tried copyediting at publishing companies but felt suffocated. He could not bear being stuffed by other people's work, force fed. He much preferred random finds, serendipitously hitting on writers who spoke to him.

His parents contributed what they could, and Camby, ironically, kept his head above water by going back to school as a teacher. An environment he hated was his support. He felt satisfaction being in control, comfortable at the head of a classroom, but he had to battle students and his rage returned. No one bothered about it as long as things ran decently. He found a little portion of the world he could manage that did not ask too much of him. Apparently teacher's rages were an acceptable part of classroom life.

Camby was not comfortable with the life he developed. Teaching was suffocating and draining. He did not like the person he became in the classroom but could not come up with anything better. He got crushes on students, spent hours fantasizing about them. Finally, he had a brief affair with a fellow teacher that ended badly and plunged him into pain he didn't expect.

It was a vulnerable time, moving toward adulthood, feeling nothing was working, falling into pain he could not get out of. It got so bad he often missed school and eventually was fired. A psychiatrist prescribed medication that helped, but a taste of such sudden and immense and lasting pain changed his view of himself. He now regarded himself as dangerous, someone to run away from. He never wanted to feel such pain again, yet he knew it was there, a possibility. As a writer, ought he close doors of self?

When we met, Camby supported himself substitute teaching. He felt less trapped by work but hated it. He could, at least, turn down jobs if he felt like resting or writing or meeting women. Meeting women was a top priority. My suspicion was that he, partly, used bouquets of women to regulate pain. Having lots of women makes losing one less dreadful and makes it easier to be lighter and freer with any one.

Camby was in conflict about medication. "My psychiatrist tells me I have a chemical imbalance and may need to take medication the rest of my life. Is that so? I'm afraid to be off it but afraid to stay on it too. I want to feel everything I am. I don't want to be afraid of myself the rest of my life. But I don't want to fall into pain I can't get out of."

There is never-ending pain in life. I feel it part of me, part of the way life is. Each person has to speak for him- or herself. My truth is that pain and bliss are mixed together. Camby's truth—

isn't that what therapy is about? I have no way of knowing if Camby suffers from a permanent chemical imbalance. Medication helped him get through a bad time. Will he need it forever? Can anyone know? Perhaps he will need it from time to time. Perhaps he will always need it. Perhaps something further will happen, and he will never need it again. It is hard to enough to work with what is happening now and do justice to it.

Camby tried therapists before me. Perhaps he needs to feel he is not trapped, bouquets of therapists. Perhaps he needs to play one against another, dilute relationships, end to try again. Perhaps starting-stopping, never getting too far, is an index of trauma, very tender tissue. When I see Camby, I wish him well, aware any visit may be his last.

Soon after we started, his freer feeling with women appeared, as if out of nowhere. Suddenly he was meeting women, a taste of success. It was as if my acceptance of his "disability" had a releasing effect. He substituted having different women for different therapists — with much more pleasure. Perhaps polygamy with them enabled monogamy with me.

The release was dramatic, and I did not analyze it away. It was, I felt, something to live through, learn from.

Some of my thoughts, fantasies:

1. Therapeutic megalomania and/or reality: If I tune into my chest, I hear something like, "Yea. Wow. You're beautiful. You're alive. I pray you grow well. I don't know what I can do for you, whether you should be here. But you *are* here. And I do feel joyous love radiating in my heart or wherever it may be. A kind of emotional field we grow in, our great petri dish. Some of its waves are lapping you and you are wading in."
2. Fields of pain. Trauma. Injury before you were born, injury while you were born, and all through the years afterward. Pain and joy make my head spin. I can't see through them. They are in my body or body soul. I feel you inside me, but

terms like "inside-outside" do not do. You are fighting to be free. Not just free of me or you. It is another kind of freedom. You taste it any way you can, but it has a lot of growing to do.

3. Love laps pain. Pain is never-ending, but love is the greater infinity, greater context. Is this a matter of faith or experience? A faith that *is* experience?

4. Argument: "Love is painful. One suffers love. Loveless pain is threatened by painful love. The loveless abyss recoils at love's entry before surrendering. But a part holds back. A small part never lets go, never gives in." Counter-argument: "Yes, of course. Make room. Still, love's core is joy."

5. A mixture of curiosity, interest. How does this happen? Someone sitting in my chair functions as a kind of background support, and Camby is released into living. What *is* going on? How does this work? What can we learn about such powerful forces? Anything may take a destructive turn any moment. Developmental faith is assailed by realistic pessimism. But none of us need be confined by simple alternatives.

6. I turn my mind-soul over in my hand and look at the imprint, a question that cannot be rubbed off, "What will happen next?" It is a question that continues after breath stops.

Where does Camby go while I think these things?

He, too, is waiting for the next pulsation, more fascinating and inclusive than rage or sullen numbing, a more pressing thirst.

GOOD FEELINGS

"It's lifting!" Dana has begun to say these words with increasing frequency. I began hearing them several years ago. They would die out and not be heard for months as she sank back into depression. I heard her say something like this nine years earlier, then she left therapy. As time passed, she became heavier, blacker. Dana's optimism scares me. Too often good feelings meant disaster was brewing. On the other hand, lack of good feeling was a disaster too.

Dana's second husband, Ray, was a rageful man, and she herself was rageful. She would play the victim, then rise up in rageful indignation and strike hard. She would scream at Ray with all her might. It could take months — at one time, years — for the outrage to build and break through. Long periods were filled with sulking, despondency, stagnation.

Then it began. Therapy released a monster. Dana's rages became preemptive. She was rageful in her own right, not simply reactive to her husband's controlling ways. Now he tasted what it was like to be cowed by *her* surges.

Once activated, rage never ends. It is, like other affects, infinite and makes infinite demands. Redress one injury, slight, abuse, mishap and others rush in. It quiets for a while, like sex or hunger, then gradually builds, exploding over a critical limen. Rage addicts might say, "This is the last time. Just once more and it's over." They may, as with masturbating, feel ashamed, or feel, in the aftermath, such an extreme could not happen again.

Just as often, ragers feel justified. They may be plugged into a God-image and believe they are righting a cosmic wrong connected with personal injury. Dana felt she was right to protect herself, to fight back and make sure she got respect. Ray did not listen. He hammered. A sense of injustice ignited her, but she was at a loss to know where such fury came from. It seemed as if God's wrath and hers were one.

Might and weakness. Victim and avenger. Educational rage—the other needs to learn a lesson. Transformational rage—the other needs to change. Battle rage—who controls whom? Domination rage, subservience rage. Will over will. Needy rage.

Isn't God always angry about injustice, some failure to be good, obedient, holy, caring? Dana gained power from God's rage released through her psyche.

At the same time, rage has a history. God's rage lives through a family. Dana's father catalogued life's injustices, incessantly enumerating how man wronged man. His rage came out in acerbic readings of daily events and history's evils. Not that he was wrong about what he saw. But to poison the mind of a child? To oppress a little girl with life's evils in ways that make her feel obscenely helpless? Dana's father did nothing about the state of affairs he bemoaned, inspiring paralysis rather than action. Life was something to rail against, not live. One does best to cast a critical eye and step aside. Dana's father's self-control was a source of pride, but he did not see that he was heightening his daughter's fear of life.

And yet, as if in a vacuum, a parenthesis, Dana's father intermittently raged against her transgressions. Angry outbursts came from nowhere. It could be that she ripped his newspaper, got too dirty, annoyed her mother. She was not supposed to notice his fits. She was supposed to benefit from them. It was as if, to some extent, he tried to correct the evils of the world by correcting minor faults of hers. His paralyzed rage at life would, without warning, seek refuge in her.

He made his living as a government accountant who felt stifled by the security he sold out to. He lived in readiness to pounce on abuse of law or simply to catch ignorance and error. He sought nourishment from family but brought poison home. His dark rage had roots reaching back to poisoning processes in his own infancy, passing through him to the next generation, drawing power from the love it mixed with.

Dana's mother did motherly things at home but was concerned more with how things looked than with how they felt. A clean house, a neat body, getting chores done, doing what one was supposed to, being good: this is what she tried to pass on to her daughter. Dana felt stifled by love, starved for feeling. It was an ethos where girls were good but boys could be bad, and her brother went on, so far as Dana was concerned, to become an obnoxious businessman.

Sometimes suffocating atmospheres are so oppressive they compress unlived feeling into a kind of dense underlayer. It is an odd but shrewd property of life that waste can be fertilizing, and some creatures, like rats or flies, find nourishment in it. Fecal odors arouse interest, as well as repugnance, partly because of the nostalgia for nourishment that went into them. Emotional toxins, especially poisoned love, can be powerful, binding nourishment. They may destroy life before releasing it, but sheer density of compressed emotions can act as a seedbed awaiting awakening.

Dana broke out in adolescence. She recoiled from her parents, feared she would be like them, and sought freedom. Her compacted underlife exploded sexually, and she slept around shotgun style, alive through massive dispersal. The fact that most of her relationships were unsatisfactory did not slow her down, in fact sped her up. The less sexual satisfaction she had, the more she tried. The idea of it turned her on. She was anything but what her parents wanted her to be. Not the mind her father wished for, not the lady of her mother's dreams.

Some of the boys she slept with were involved in theater, and she began singing and acting with them. Here was a real high. For a time she felt released. She threw herself into roles, sang at parties. The first major crash came after high school graduation. Her crowd vanished, her supports, imaginary or real, gone. Sex, with its lack of emotional and physical satisfaction, was not enough to support her, and she suffered her first depressive collapse. Her parents came to her aid—itself a defeat—and found psychiatric help. With some supportive therapy and medication, she was able to move on.

After a period of not knowing what to do, trying and hating several jobs, she joined an acting class. It dawned on her this was the one thing she had really enjoyed in high school. She might or might not be an actress, but her happiest moments had come when she was acting. Within weeks she had sex with her drama teacher, and in a year she married him. In three years she mothered two children, whom her husband could not support. She could not sustain being a working mother—and hating her jobs, which paid little, didn't help.

Her husband was a brilliant actor who never lacked roles in local plays. He was doing what he loved and felt money would come—if it didn't, there was love. On this he was uncompromising. He loved his children and felt they would grow like flowers. Money was less important than living naturally. But most of the real-time child care fell on Dana, and it was she who had to make ends meet. Her own acting time withered and her insistence that her husband do more to help fell on deaf ears.

Her rages began and got nowhere. She became afraid she would kill her children. She found herself hovering over them with a knife in her hand. When this happened repeatedly, she tried hiding knives from herself, but found them in her hand again. Almost to protect her children, she fell into profound depression and did nothing. Periods of sadness were short-lived. Her weeping transformed from pain over her condition to a kind of blank stare and empty trance. She sat near her youngest child for hours in a vacuous state, not knowing what to do. Her husband looked the other way, not so much pretending it wasn't happening, as being absorbed in his own active, get-out-of-the-house sort of blankness. She became inert, he hyperactive. She couldn't get out of the house, he couldn't stay in it.

One day he returned to an empty house. The children were with her parents, while she was receiving psychiatric help. She never returned to him, and he could scarcely believe she had the strength to leave.

To make a go of it on her own seemed impossible, but she found ways to do it. Her parents sometimes helped, her ex-husband sometimes took the children, friends helped. But mainly she did it herself, barely. She found therapists and eventually formed an attachment with one who she felt believed in her. After ten years, he moved to France, and she plunged into free fall.

Depression was a constant. It was never absent for long, not since her first breakdown after high school. Therapy helped to modulate it, especially the effects of her ten-year attachment to the man who left. Survival was her focus, but she had integrity too. Her long therapy helped her focus on a range of feelings to balance depressive pain, but the latter pulled on her and she succumbed to orgies of self-hate. She feared that her self-hate polluted her children, but there was little she could do, except keep trying. Therapy insisted she have faith in herself, but the pain of being spoke louder. When her therapist left, the brakes were gone.

When I met Dana, pain oscillated with emptiness. It was difficult to tell which was the baseline. Did pain arise from emptiness or emptiness turn off the pain? She wanted so badly to die. She looked back at the rubble of her life. Her former husband drowned, no one knows whether accidentally or not. Her father died soon afterward. She managed to hold her children above the rising waters long enough for them to reach adulthood and begin the business of saving themselves. Her mother now needed care that Dana could not give her. Dana married again, to a sensitive, rageful, worried man, Ray, who made a living. She would be with someone who could not sit still, when she needed lots of time to herself.

It eventually dawned on Dana that she tried to use Ray's rage to substitute for depression. She could point and say, "Look how bad he is." Fury at him distracted her from herself. It was also true that his tyranny fueled her depression. Many women would have left and felt better. But Dana knew she tried to escape through his badness, and that she was miserable in her own right. She was wretched before him and would be wretched after him. Was the wretchedness of staying together a better or worse kind of misery?

She even felt in his rage a kind of aliveness, an aliveness she would come to feel in her rage as well. Rage resonated with rage. She wondered if he and she were mirror images—he anxious, she depressed. She was angry at him for being an anxious person, he at her for being depressed. Dana, too, was angry at herself for being depressed, while Ray was angry at himself for being fearful. Rage gave dependency something to organize around, providing an illusion of strength, perpetuating trauma. Dana and Ray shared a sense of catastrophe. Both were serious worriers. For her, depressive collapse was ever imminent, and all the rage in the world could do little to offset it. Rage was smoke, craters of depression real fire.

"It's lifting—after thirty years, more." Should I be apprehensive, terrified like Ray? Is the rise of good feelings a measure of the fall to come?

"Ever since I remember, I've heard the negative voice and thought it was me. It tells me whatever I'm doing is bad—I'm no good as a student, a wife, a mother, a person. For a moment I felt happy acting in high school, then it died. It was killed by life, my husband, caring for children, my own awfulness. It got shot down by the voice that says, 'You're no good. They're putting up with you for sex or because you take care of things or because no one better is around.'

"An old friend I ran into yesterday told me about a theater group she belongs to. They put on plays, readings, things. They do it because they want to, not because of money. They try to make ends meet. My heart leaped when I heard about it, and we spoke about giving it a try. The negative voice started to say I was no good and it wouldn't work, but my heart screamed out, 'You're not me. You're not the me I love.' Love? Love?

"Where does love come from? Where did *this* love come from? Suddenly—it happened like that—the bad voice felt foreign, something grafted, a substance my system rejected. I didn't know I could reject it and not pretend. That's not exactly right. It was not me rejecting it. My being, my whole being felt differently in that instant. There wasn't room for the bad voice then. There was no real place for it. Before it took all my space. It was the only place to live, so living was awful. Now another space appeared, another place entirely, like waking in a new country. Free, really me. The bad dream—I was out of it."

Moments of grace knitted together. "When I acted in high school and a teacher supported me and friends helped—if the rest of my life had been half as good, it would have been terrific. My first baby, the baby I wanted, my body works, unconditional love, joy terrific. I used to sing when I was a kid, quiet singing to myself, and I could feel my voice tingling through my skin and insides. I wonder if I had my first orgasm singing? The thrill meeting my first husband, his acting class, passport to another universe, the true one. My therapist who made me feel moments of faith—moments that broke and are coming back now."

The best moments of Dana's life found each other—the good thread, the radiance. Then fear. "I'm afraid of the good stuff. I'll undo the clearing, the negative voice will take over. I'm afraid Ray will die if I get any happier. Something awful will happen to my kids. Christ died. He felt abandoned. I fear being abandoned, abandoning the negative voice. And a deeper fear I've not known —abandoning the good, being abandoned by it. Double dreads in all directions. I fear too much good and the revenge of the negative.

"All my life I believed in Good Friday, not Easter. The negative death voice. I was so mad at God that every bit of love hurt. Wherever there is love, something breaks. Love never goes right for me. Any kind of love, parent love, love for kids, work, other people— love means hurt, something awful happening, getting set for a new, unimaginable twist to an old story. There are good love moments, love without being injured—but they vanish, people go away, die. Time takes them. There are people I could be with without feeling maimed or poisoned, moments when hearts touch. But the awful thing comes. Within two days of graduating high school, the teacher who supported me in acting died in a car crash. I knew the moment he died. My heart sank, and I knew something awful happened. I'm afraid of that sinking feeling. I'm afraid I'll have it with you. Something awful will happen just as I'm coming alive. I feel love coming back and I'm afraid."

Eclipse and return of love, years between. "It's been a long dry spell—three decades—and it's over. A fifty-year-old woman coming alive. It makes me laugh to see little things different—getting gas before the gauge is on empty so I don't have to tensely wait to see whether or not I'll make it. I'd torture myself all sorts of ways. Will I get where I'm going or run out of gas? I can't stop laughing. I was stuck that way for so many years."

Dana tried medication a number of times but did not care for it. She did not like the film it put around her and some of her feelings, a platform raising her subtly. She could not ignore the sense of an intangible something between her and her, like certain people can't bear the sensation of wearing glasses (they see the rims or fuzzy doubling rather than the world). Friends told her medication changed their lives. Medication helps some of my clients a lot.

But Dana, true to her vision, got through it herself. The bubble burst. Her mind and self felt clearer than ever. The balance changed. We would learn the change was solid and definitive. She was no longer in danger of the great, airless fall. Something drove her toward herself, and she followed it all the way. She felt proud of herself and so did I. What she went through was real, not makeshift. Nevertheless, our work was far from over.

Once, when I asked her what she thought happened, how the fever broke, she mused, "Do the interpretations pile up and reach a critical mass? I have more energy than Ray now. Can it be they were adding up for years, years, years—without my knowing it?"

Psychotherapy bathes Dana in meaning. Dana has a hunger for meaning. Her love of theater is a quest for meaning. Meaning is singing. Life sings through her. Still, I feel what happened with

Dana was more than meaning, not less. She was driven to burrow into what bothered her, relentlessly. She could not let go of it, and it would not let go of her. She pile drove into the dense spot, the stuckness, and, finally, hit oil. A kind of mute "feel" led the way. Interpretation was part of it, seeping into the clot, disappearing, transforming into a kind of silent loom, knitting her together, knitting life together.

About six months after the critical turn, Dana remembers an old dream. "I was on the end of a diving board, legs not working. So I was going to dive by sitting. OK—both meanings: Yeah, I can do it, and yeah, I'm crippled. Maybe now I can stand and dive." Dana felt relief not pretending she wasn't crippled, at the same time feeling more able and ready. "It's no contradiction not being able to dive and diving." The clot was melting a little more, making room for not being able to and being able to. "I can be both. I can live, and I hold myself back. This bothness. It feels new. *I* feel new. Living bothness is finding a whole new place."

Dreams present challenges before we are ready. They signal positions we can do little about, SOS signals, expressing emotional plagues. It took many years for Dana to link up with an old dream and make room for its tensions. The making room itself felt like the start of breathing. "Experience changes like clouds, one minute this way, one minute that. How much wonderfulness can I stand?"

Burial ↔ resurrection. Previously a rise was signifier of a fall. Now it was part of a life-giving sequence, part of the richness, the brew.

We are about to part for our summer break, both of us going away. A week earlier, Dana took time off from work to visit grandchildren, something she never would have done before. "I would've been afraid of what would happen when I wasn't there, some bad thing, the work wouldn't get done, things would fall apart without me. This time it wasn't important what might go wrong in my absence. It was nice to feel how unimportant my not being there would be and let go that grippy, gooey stuff."

"The world goes on without you," I commented. "But it's fun to be there for parts of it." I added an afterthought, probably a grippy, gooey thing: "It looks like you're discovering your selector and volume control."

"I'm not supposed to be this happy," she cries. She thanks me and we hug.

**W**arren has a bee phobia. It got so bad he stayed in his apartment for days at a time, afraid to go out. When he began missing work and falling behind financially, he finally sought help.

It is something of a wonder that most people afraid to leave their homes manage to get to therapy. Both fear and strength in the face of a phobia are variable. Even with many missed sessions, therapy can go on. Today, also, work can go on via phone or computer.

I was taken by surprise when Warren appeared—more by my impressions than anything Warren said or did. His face seemed soft and flowerlike, yet there was a buzz in his eyes and a sting in his voice. I saw Warren, at once, as bee and flower, delicate and stinging.

Look what suggestibility does. I don't think this image would have come to me without knowing Warren has a bee phobia. Yet this was the first time I had such an image with a bee-phobic person. In fact, I suspect this was the first time I saw anyone as a flower-bee in just this way. Perhaps, then, there is a deeper suggestibility at work, a deeper emotional transmission involving truth needing work. It remained to be seen to what extent I was capturing a bit of Warren's soul with my mind, smearing him with my own soul colors and mental categories, or opening myself to an impact that might pay off for him.

Within seconds, I was both afraid of and wanted to protect him. If I were true to the flower-bee image, I should say I wanted to smell him, enjoy him, but feared if I drew too close, I'd get stung.

"Why shouldn't I be afraid of bees," Warren went on. "Killer bees zoom miles after you. People die of bee bites. They're all over the garbage outside. You can't go down a street or pass a corner without them being all over. You're not safe anywhere."

I tried staying responsive but my mind was cluttered, buzzing. Ideas like bees. I felt my clutter and waited. He is a bee, afraid of himself. He stings himself. He is vulnerable like a flower, but not so attractive. What does he have to offer? Can he give of himself? Is he too cluttered with panic and noise to breathe?

He tells me about his asthma. Respiratory problems began as a child. He was afraid to leave home for fear he would not be able to catch his breath. He would suffocate and die, and no one would be there to help him. No one would know what to do. He would not be able to breathe. Fear of bees and not being able to breathe seemed to go together.

Today he has medication. What if he forgets it? What if it is not strong enough? What if he cannot get to a hospital in time?

He is preoccupied with adrenal concerns. Panic spreads. It focuses for a time on breathing and bees, then spreads, then becomes concentrated again. Does he need this adrenaline hit? Does it make him feel alive? An adrenaline addict?

Is that a pejorative thought, a stinging thought, my stinging mind?

I'm flooded with images. Energy panic.

I think Warren is in a state of energy panic.

Freud was right to connect energy and anxiety. My mind travels to Freud as a point of organization, energy anxiety, mind anxiety.

God, so simple. I'm afraid of having a mind, afraid of energy.

Having a mind is too much for me. The press of energy too much.

I'm having a panic attack, panic over being alive, being real, *psyche panic,* panic over having a psyche or being psychical, sensitive. What has happened to this man's sensitivity? What has ripped it to shreds of fear?

William Blake: "Energy is Eternal Delight."

Not for Warren, not for me when I'm with Warren.

Yet Freud points out there is a kind of pleasure in the panic, pleasure in the negative, the symptom, the pain.

Perhaps this is to say one cannot succeed in totally denuding oneself either of pleasure or pain as long as one is a *psychesomatic* being, as long as one is in this universe.

Pleasure is the underside of skin.

Pleasure usually puts brakes on panic. Not so for Warren. Pleasure as a braking system is not working. I think, as I look at him, something has gone wrong, something is working to turn pleasure into pain.

I envision sources of pleasure streaming through the body, but in Warren a switch is turned and as fast as being alive potentially produces pleasure, something transforms it into panic. A pain machine.

I'm already sensing, wondering what bad things happened to this man to lacerate him so. He has become a cramped version of himself, contracted to panic, phobia, the sort of egocentricity that has one or two self-states as chronic focus.

What does Warren see when he looks at me? Can he see me? Is what he sees colored by panic? Do I become someone to hold on to, to save him, to make the bad stuff go away? Someone to push away as part of the bad stuff?

Panic everywhere.

Where do *I* come in?

Right now I need to wait, to be there, to feel the pressure not to be there, the pressure to be obliterated, the pressure to be everything.

Writing this becomes a kind of time machine, or the kind of cinematography that strings together different moments of a flower's growth, from seed to cessation, semblance of a lifetime in a few minutes.

Within a few weeks, pictures of the sort I expected took form. Father away on business trips a lot, drank too much, easily angered. Once Warren woke up to strange sounds and found his father pissing on the living room floor, blotto, in a semistuporous rage, piteous, terrifying. His legs, barely supporting his fury, threatened to give way under him. Such a mixture of weakness and rage—a man a thread away from collapsing, shoring himself up with self-pitying anger, a stinging, wrenching sight.

Poisoned-poisoning phallic stinger. Instead of father, gateway to the symbolic dimension, a debased, frightening image of trauma. More than image or representation, for trauma spreads through one's being, muscles, breathing, neurons. Trauma becomes cellular. It is in the way skin feels, the tightness in one's face, a constriction of one's feelings, an arched back, pains in one's body.

It is not memory waiting for uncovering or covering. It is memory that stays there, not going anywhere, radiating trauma. Even as it fades, effects of what led to it go on silently in the background, inhibiting movement, words, gestures, touch. One feels oneself living in a state of semiparalysis.

It won't do to say that was then, this is now. I was terrified of my father, but not everyone is my father, and I need not be terrified now. To the extent this is helpful, fine. But there is more than words can reach in one's nerves, chemistry, vision, and sense of life. Not simply that trauma was then, and now is another day. Trauma waves spread through the present and are part of one's feel for life.

One tries to circumscribe and limit traumatized states: attach them to images, representations, memories, past events. I am afraid because...Reasons help somewhat, but fear goes on. A stinging penis is one such signifier. It gives to injury a local habitation, a handle. One can try to make oneself bigger than what happened. But since what happened is now part of self, one keeps trying to become bigger than oneself. To become more than the sum of one's trauma, to become bigger, to transcend oneself, to build up tolerance for oneself: pain and fear and fury push one on.

It takes years for Warren to begin to realize he is here now and no amount of talking about the past will free him from it. He is here now with his fears.

But talk is not all vain. He must let me know about his mother too, perhaps foremost. Who was more devastating, mother or father? Who wins the trauma prize? There is a push toward and away from truth, to tell the truth, share the truth, as well as glamorize it. This happened to me, this is the way it was. I'm hysterical and dead, unable to move and unable to stop moving, a bug wriggling in a stone. Frozen rage, dread, injury: me. Me stuck in a frozen sea of turbulence. Vanity, vanity—but not all vanity.

Freud wrote of war victims dreaming repeatedly of scenes that traumatized them. It is not simply that they could not let go of what happened. What happened could not let go of them. Like images of war scenes, compilations of mothering moments mesmerized and silenced Warren. Shell shock. Not simply so that truth sets you free. Truth binds, scars, maims, blows holes in you. The drive to share the truth of one's life, document it, brand it with another subjectivity, makes therapy real. One hopes there is something in this realness that makes blowing oneself up freeing.

There may have been a time when Warren's mother felt good enough to him. But he does not remember such a time. Good moments were marred by temper, agitation, withdrawal, self-absorption, neglect. She lay in bed hallucinating, weeping, angry. When Warren was a little older, she busied herself with work, went her own way, found him a nuisance. He spent a lot of time alone, trying to soothe himself. When he went to school, she was critical of him. There was not much he could do right.

He felt victimized by both parents yet was certain they loved him. They probably loved him without having the ability to back love up, lacking parental resources. Love fused with toxic elements, toxic love. He was subject to the uncontrollable in their personalities, their inability to get out of themselves. He was subject to the same forces in them to which they were subject themselves—except he was their child. They were probably waiting for a good childhood themselves, trapped in a doomed one. The household lacked a personality capable of struggling with itself enough to make a difference. So many people waiting to be a child to someone. Yet Warren grew up, became a moderately successful businessman, partly surviving the background that maimed him. Stinging hole, stinging nipple, stinging self.

Maybe Warren was being the injured stay-at-home mother waiting for help. Maybe Warren's mother imagined he would help, a messiah child undoing wound and disability. Marriage didn't cure her, maybe motherhood would. This is the way life works: one stays at home until one finds a better mother. Home is a garden growing mothers until one works, growing babies until one works.

Frozen rage mothers.

Frozen rage babies.

Warren seemed proud of staying at home. He seemed bigger in an apartment than in the world. He seemed ashamed of getting to my office, fearful I might say, "You see, you can do it." Fearful I might turn him against himself.

Pride in being unable to? Freedom from a growing link with me? He likes our crazy talk together. It competes with the pleasure of being afraid. What is all this talk about mothers, babies, wounds, and nipples? The mad talk of therapy, another kind of *jouissance*. Another kind of pissing on the floor. Someone actually seeing the terror in skin.

My tongue is a stinging nipple. Honey therapy stings.

I promise I will not try to get him better.

"Then what am I coming for?"

"My guess is you're coming to see what it's like for us to be together, to hang out and talk and feel the surprise of what happens when we chat, argue, grow silent, see the unseeable. Maybe you come to have a moment of not being you."

"I come to prove I can."

"And then recover a lifetime?"

"I come instead of climbing Mt. Everest."

"Mt. Everest is easier."

"At least I get out of bed, out of my apartment."

He is proud of getting to my office. It does help, doesn't it, that so much of what we do together is about him? Where else can he get this? The me-ness of therapy, isn't that an attraction, in some way empowering?

Getting to my office is a bit like getting out of mother, getting into him.

Is there a difference between his and mother's rage, his and mother's wounds?

Getting to therapy creates a bridge, a stretch. Moving from there to here is more than physical movement.

Is there much difference between mother and father? Have they collapsed into each other through the violence of trauma? Mother dreads, father dreads?

Rage spreads through the body. The body tries to absorb it, recoiling, shutting down, hiding. Can a body become invisible? Is that part of what not being outside tries to do? It fails, as the body grows bigger between walls. Body grows, insides shrink.

What sorts of insides pulse in therapy?

Believe it or not, there are times therapy is fun for a phobic person. Some people feel more pain in therapy than anywhere else, as if all the pain in their beings gets concentrated in therapy. It is a horror to come to sessions and a relief to get out. For Warren, though, therapy was a relief, a sort of home away from home, another place he could go and be afraid.

It was important for me not to be too obtrusive. It's hard to describe how I played myself down. The gesture was quite spontaneous, as if I sensed Warren couldn't take anything too hurtful or acutely real. The real I offered was a primary process blend. It sounds scary to say that as soon as Warren entered the room he saw that mental processes here were more important than bodies. Yet, for Warren, this felt good, a kind of soul sigh, "at last—insides spilling everywhere." And for moments, that everywhere was me.

You might think it unpleasant or threatening to lend yourself to another ego. Sometimes this is so. But there can be pleasure in becoming a kind of sensitive substrate, welcoming another's impact, being background film for another's unconscious. It feels good not being one's ordinary self and giving oneself over to therapy's altered state. Maybe actors share this bliss, taking on another self, entering a role, becoming larger by seeking a vanishing point. Mothers must share it when they meld with an infant, letting the other's needs dominate awhile.

It doesn't take long to meld in therapy and feel more comfortable with a patient than with the "outside" world. You and the patient share altered states. You are alone together, focused on self. Only insides are real — feelings, thoughts, images, psychic flow. If one speaks of the weather or a baseball game, one works with emotional fields. "It is ghastly outside, an electric storm, breathtaking though!" "The Mets lost last night in the bottom of the ninth!" Small talk deals with destructive forces, the question of what makes life worth living, takes psychic temperature, mediates emotional balance.

I become afraid of the outside world. I never want to leave therapy. I want Warren to stay forever. It feels better in therapy than anywhere else. I can't wait for Warren to leave. I want to be alone. I want to take a walk, go to a movie, say hello to my wife. I'll be lost forever if Warren stays a moment longer. I want it ended this instant. I want it to go on and on, a song I want to play forever. The therapy womb. I never want to be born. A therapy parasite. I've found a host in Warren. A moment's peace feeling his pain, his hopes. I've escaped. A moment's concentration, immersion in psychic life. Time ruptures it. We leave each other until the next session, insides ruptured, held together by the feeling we have when we're together.

My trance is broken by Warren going on about stinging nipples. Rather, one trance is exchanged for another. He is picturing himself as a baby sucking on nipple bees. He stops breathing. He imagines more pain than he feels, pain about to come. He is in a state of shock. His moving mouth suddenly stops. Milk mixed with stinging pain, pain all over. Mouth pain spreading everywhere instantaneously. Nourishment with shock and pain. Movement permeated by frozenness. Bees move, turning from honey makers to warriors. They sting and sting and sting. Warren can't stop sucking. He needs nourishment. Does he begin to imagine stinging is nourishment?

The world becomes a stinging nipple. Nourishment is stinging. Pain is nourishment. He can't stop seeking nourishing pain.

Warren begins to feel the world is stopping, Armageddon near. He does not know what to do with frozen rage. He cannot bear it. He dreads thawing out. Every flower is rageful. Flowers are stinging bees. Breasts kill. Where did softness go?

He touches his mouth. It is still there, but he cannot feel it. His hand goes to his chest, his heart. Nothing important there, barely a body.

He is in a world where nourishment maims. It is the way things are.

This goes on for many sessions, off and on. He cannot wait for his next session to see what will happen to him. There is no other place he can go like this. Who would listen, let it happen? Who would feel it? When one asks if a falling tree makes a sound if no one hears it, is one also asking what becomes of feeling if no one responds?

One day Warren's back tingles when he speaks. Pleasure spreads. He begins to share more. He comes alive beyond the panic rush. Other feelings catch his attention, evoke interest. He wants to talk about everything he sees. Bees begin to fade. He looks fuller, stronger, as if life has a chance.

# GLASS HOUSE

"People who live in glass houses shouldn't throw stones," Dan says. "Not for reasons one usually thinks. Not because someone would retaliate, throw stones back. Not a do unto others thing. It's worse than that, way worse. You could break the walls yourself. Shatter your own glass." He is quiet awhile, waves of silence. In the silence I feel stones, glass, images of shatter. Different kinds of shatter. Cracks like water making paths in sand. I picture myself as a child pouring buckets of water in the sand, helping to form pathways and being surprised by them. Explosive shatter, a glass unexpectedly exploding when you touch it or pour something too hot or cold in it, when contrasts are too great. The Crystal Night in Germany when glass turned into skulls. And my job, breaks inside skulls.

I remember having trouble with the glass house saying as a kid. Friends explained it to me until I finally got the normative meaning. But there was some background mystery—if you're in a glass house, wouldn't it break if you threw stones? Was I feeling what Dan now explains to me? A life encased by glass? I locate the film, the gauze in my head in childhood, cotton still there. My friends got outside the gauze and could see in. They were outside the glass looking in. They could take in both views, and understand immediately that someone in a glass house was subject to injury. While Dan and I were stuck inside, cracking our shells without getting out.

"You know, the bell jar," he said, thinking of Sylvia Plath. I thought of Freud's wolf man, the caul, the veil between himself and the world.

"Are thoughts thrown against the glass or part of the glass itself?" Dan asks.

"You dare not move too quickly, inner or outer movement," I said. "It is always dangerous."

"It is dangerous if the glass shatters, dangerous if it doesn't," Dan said, alarmed and resigned.

After a pause, he continues. "Do you understand? It is awful when it shatters because it lets other people in. Like cracks in the atmosphere. I will be poisoned by ozone. I am in a glass house, like a greenhouse, because you are too dangerous. People are killers."

"Yes, I am wounding," I say.

"But also soothing. Your voice makes me feel good."

"I make you feel good and I hurt you."

"Yes."

Quiet again. I start thinking about how they can make glass that's hard to break today. They even use it for walls of homes. "You know, I get the idea you're afraid the glass will never break, that you cannot break it no matter how hard you try. You'll be stuck inside breathing your own breath if ventilation breaks down."

I'm thinking of Bion's surgical shock image, the emotional corollary to bleeding to death in your own arteries. Psychic space expands, explodes, becomes so vast and void that any feeling beginning to appear in it thins, becomes too diffuse to be felt in a meaningful way. I also think of a woman in group therapy who felt she spoke so loudly she feared she was screaming, while group members thought she spoke normally or had trouble hearing her.

"Maybe you feel I'm like glass that cannot break and will not register the impact of your words, your being. And maybe you fear I'll break too easily."

"It is both, you know, it is both," Dan responds. "It is worse than you imagine. Or maybe you do know, after all. It sounds like you may. The glass is a kind of double skin. A double casing. No air comes through. I can't get out of it, nor can I get through to you. It is, too, an outside skin you can't penetrate. It keeps you out. It keeps me in. It is like being in a soundproof closet no one knows exists.

"Yet we are speaking and we are feeling. You are getting through to me and I to you."

I know Dan is right. We are communicating, feeling each other. We are speaking about noncommunicating, being permanently removed and shut out. We are experiencing both at once. He is telling me how painful and safe and dangerous it is to be alone in a cut-off way. And yet we are not alone.

"My glass is always breaking and never broken," he goes on. "It's endlessly frustrating. I can't get out or into myself. I can't reach or find myself or you. At the same time, I come here and tell you about it and you talk to me and stay with me. It is like you are with someone in a coma, trying to feed him vibes so he can know someone is there, something good or real is there.

"I've gotten so far I can contact a place where feelings come from. A flow of pleasure, happiness, irritability, anger, fury, sadness, a lot of fear. A river of feelings. My little feeling box inside my little house. I don't know if I'm feeling feelings about anything or whether they just come and go.

"It's taken a long time for me to get to this. There used to be nothing. The next step is not just to feel but feel about something. My feelings are muffled inside the enclosure, the glass house. I want the muffledness to break or dissolve.

"I used to scream. I was in a therapy where we screamed, kicked, tried to be a baby letting it all out completely. It was good. Sometimes I felt in the clear, through the wall. Then the fog reformed and I'd get heavy again, same me, stuck inside the glass. What used to be a greenhouse became darker, less and less light got in. I tried to make it brighter inside myself, my inside light. You know, we have light inside, many lights, holy flame, eternal light, Chanukah lights burning on and on. But they need light from outside too and air. They get dim if there's nothing but your own breathing.

"Rage didn't help. I thought it did. I felt stronger. I felt my body more, screaming strength. But I couldn't keep it up. You can't scream all the time. You fade. You need to rest. You go away. You die out and sometimes not all of you comes back.

"That's what I feel here, more of me coming back, more of me missing. At least when I'm here I can begin to feel the missing, the filling, the fading, the returning. So there is life between rages.

"My rages charge me. Like electrical infusions. All that screaming energy, so much at once. Then subsiding, recuperating, quieter. Rage does help.

"Rage helps and harms.

"When I was in scream therapy I used to scream at girlfriends. I threatened to hit one and almost did. I grazed her face. It was part of my scream. I felt it was part of therapy. I would feel cowardly if I didn't do it. I hated her that moment. I was furious. I pictured striking her, getting her to feel me, give more of herself. She seemed so remote, staring at me far away.

"I felt right to do it, justified. I felt myself all in my mind seeing her remove herself and thinking I've got to get her to respond. Somehow I got the idea my rage would bring us closer. Warm rage. Cold Rage. My whole being in it. She would feel all the me I could get into it. It would make things intimate. She would feel more of me, more for me.

"I never expected her to recoil in horror and get mad and break off with me. She acted afraid instead of warm. She was furious and gave me a tongue lashing and screamed and left. Instead of making everything better, everything was worse. Broken. I damaged her feelings and our relationship beyond repair. How can this be? You feel in your mind something compelling and true, and it turns out the worst thing you can do. It turns out true for you but no one else.

"It's hard to believe what feels so right for you is wrong for someone else. I couldn't take it in. It cracked the glass, yet the glass wouldn't crack. My therapist tried to tell me you do things in therapy that won't work outside. You can't go around screaming and expecting people to like you for it. So I wonder, if therapy is a world apart, how does it carry over? How can it help?

"I know I shouldn't blame therapy, but when I lost my girlfriend, I thought this therapy is wrecking my chances at living.

( *Glass House* : 103 )

I've got to find something else. I've got to stop menacing people, scaring myself. I was a raw mess."

"You needed to regroup, reset yourself," I say. "You needed to see if there was more to life than wrecking things."

"What does one do with the me- and you-ness of things? How does one take this in? I can feel something so powerfully but then have to draw back and think, well, what are *you* feeling? Yet I have to feel what I'm feeling. I have to—I don't know—make room for it. It puzzles me. Don't I have to find some way to express it, to make it real, to give it its due? If I just ignore it or note it or let it be, won't it disappear? Won't a part of me vanish? Won't *I* vanish?"

"What about now?" I ask. "We're talking now. We're listening now. "

"I'm torn. What I like is you don't try to pin me. You don't say this is you and that's that. You don't say that's the real thing and that isn't. You seem to take it all as real, as something to think about. It's like you're saying my feelings are real and not real at the same time. I mean, not that they're unreal. But part of a larger scene, part of something that's bigger, and more are coming. But when we speak, I can't feel all of me. But now I'm wondering if there's an all of me to feel. It's always this and that or this or that. It goes on and on, yet I am real. I'm here looking for help, trying to live. I'm here gasping, struggling for breath. And you sit there breathing."

"I'm not struggling?"

"You don't get into it like I do. You seem to rise above the damage."

"I don't get hurt?"

"I think you do sometimes. I hear it in your voice, I see you flinch, tighten, but you—I don't know—you sit and come back. I don't know what you do. You seem to be able to take care of yourself."

"You're not too much for me?"

"I'm afraid of that. Too much for anyone."

"You wreck everything you touch. You leave damage in your wake."

"That's what I'm afraid of."

"You'll wreck your feeling for me, like you wrecked your girlfriend's feeling for you."

"Or you'll do something wrong I can't let go, and I won't be able to stay because things went bad."

"Like your girlfriend left you."

"Yes. People don't recover from each other. Things don't go on. There is a rage inside or a void that makes life impossible."

My mind goes back to the glass house and wonders if it forms as protection against rage and void, to bind them, keep them in or out. Or whether it comes because support for interflow is lacking and rage arises to penetrate it, create flow. Dan describes both, no either-or. But rage and void seem linked.

We're quiet. I feel myself start to smile. He beams. "It's totally glorious, isn't it," I say.

He is beaming, tears streaming, sparkling.

TRUE SELF AND MURDER

**B**urt lived what people would think of as a full life. Wonderful family, successful and fascinating work, country home, travels. He was attractive, took good care of himself, had many skills. From the outside, an enviable life, a good life. On a number of occasions he mentioned he'd envy himself, if he didn't know himself.

He knew himself too well, unfortunately the wrong self, the sick self—which felt to him like the only self, the real one.

Many people want to contact their true selves, not thinking it could be truly awful. What if it turns out the true self is sick, warped, deformed—bent out of shape forever?

Viewpoint 1 (V-1): The warped self is developmental mishap, true self traumatized, gone wrong. With help, it can be whole again.

Viewpoint 2 (V-2): Don't be Pollyannaish. No one fully recovers. Wholeness is too much to ask. One gets better in some ways that can make a difference. But there are still crippled, paralyzed areas.

Viewpoint 3 (V-3): Idiots. The true self is ruthless—driven. It lusts for power, being on top—it is ambitious, envious, wrathful, cunning.

V-1: If people weren't so badly injured, there would be more love in the world. Or perhaps I should say it the other way: if there were more love, there'd be less injury and warp.

V-3: Do you want to love lust and power out of existence? Where would vitality stream from?

V-2: You're both losing perspective, too one-sided. Keep a balanced view. It's not one or the other. There are many tendencies, urges, possibilities. We are woven by and weave many-stranded baskets. Remember Ecclesiastes, rhythm, timeliness? Buddha, the middle way? Survival, triumph, integrity—conflicting blends, raw materials up for grabs, always fresh challenges.

Burt: "I just want to murder you. How dare you wipe me out? Your laughing arrogance."

Burt says this to all the voices, the rudimentary democracy of the soul. They are all scavengers, misbegotten, up to no good. They don't understand a thing. And if they are up to some good, all the worse. They go unheeded, unfelt, beyond the pale.

Is Burt speaking to me? To his parents? To missing parts of self? To the world?

Now in child's skin, aiming mainly at parents: "I wanted to kill them but there was nothing I could do to them. I could not make them stop, feel what I felt, be different. All I could do was sustain endless defeat, no potency." So it is a power matter—power of big people, powerlessness of little ones.

All that feels real is the wish to murder.

"In sex I press down excruciatingly on her clitoris, yet this bonds us, makes her be mine through pain."

Pain bonds. Murder bonds. Sex is a kind of murder. Perhaps, too, murder a kind of sex.

"Will you forgive me for this? I can't stop it." Is he asking me, her, some cosmic other, something missing? Who has authority? He makes it clear he is now a child asking his parents to forgive him for his hatred of them. He feels this as imperative.

"I never even knew the child needs forgiveness for wanting to do this for his mother—to his mother. My father went to the grave hating me—and me hating him. They owed that to me, to forgive me for what I wanted to do to them."

It suddenly feels as if Burt has found a secret, a secret place of needing to be forgiven as a child for wanting to kill, to injure, to bond through pain.

————————

Burt: "Tell me how to appreciate and use this precious gift."
He is speaking of life and creativity

( *True Self and Murder* : 107 )

Burt: "I hate it. [He means life, creativity, but veers into hating the blindness of people]. Stupid God and people concerned with what and when to eat and fuck and pray and rest or wear. Not the wounding. Schizophrenics are lucky. It shows. Being schizophrenic simplifies things. Everyone knows you're sick. But the wounding that goes on—everyone turns their backs on or pretends not to see. No one wants to know. Maybe no one knows what to do with it—that would be OK, an admission, a start. But not to want to know—not caring, not being able to begin to care what we do to each other and ourselves—the real thing. Everyone does things for ulterior motives. There's no love in the universe?

"I hate myself talking to you. What's *my* ulterior motives?

"It's a beautiful day. I can identify it but not feel it. I can see this is a day people call beautiful, and I can call it beautiful too. But I lack sensory feeling of it. Instead, I have a scary feeling in my rectum, nausea. That's what's real for me, not the beautiful day. How can I communicate that? How do I tell people about my frightened ass?"

He is telling me, of course. But lacks feeling of that too. Lacks feeling of me feeling or hearing or validating or recognizing anything about him at all.

"I have a confession to make. When I woke up this morning, my voice was sonorous. It sounded full and sonorous in my own ears. I could feel it. I liked the way I looked in the mirror, too. This happens sometimes but is mainly new. For a time I was not an amorphous blob of energy. Will it do any good? Will it hold up or lead to anything or make a difference? I couldn't feel the day, but I felt me, my sound and sight. So I do have outside and inside. It happens. I know this is because I talk to you, and you are there even if I say I cannot feel any of this. I do not feel any of this. But for a moment I am real or partly real. When I woke up this morning I felt beautiful, the sight and sound of me beautiful. It will fade. It must fade. It may come back. I'm afraid to say this, as you and I will make too much of it or too little or do something wrong with it, and I'm afraid you will think me too narcissistic or lost.

But I am narcissistic and lost. You're going to kill me for having something good."

There is a murderer in the room, a potential murderer. For the moment, at least, there is something good to murder. The murder has an aim. It is not simply wholesale obliteration of good and bad. It is focused.

D. W. Winnicott writes of latent memory of a fading scream as the self fades out of existence. His patient little by little finds the fading scream as she and it drop into fathomless silence. Burt seems preoccupied with frozen murder more than with fading scream, although the sessions are a kind of murderous-murdered scream. Our sessions are an act of murder screaming for help, a murder screaming for recognition.

Yet recognition seems to go unfelt. No matter how much recognition, the murderous scream goes on. Then one morning, outside of our sessions, an act of beauty, perception of beauteous self or sight and sound of self. He knows it will be murdered but begins to think it will come back—life after death. Perhaps he senses someday it will spread, that it already is spreading.

What is important to recognize is an ever present murder. Burt sees this murder everywhere. People doing it to each other, babies, children, themselves. How can therapy escape murder—how can he or I go on after a session, after death or mutilation?

He will remain a furious murderer and victim until everyone on earth sees that murder is alive. How did a moment of beauty escape?

I see a baby hiding from the sight and sound of a mother it cannot stand and who cannot stand it. "I can't stand it," is a parental cry. Parents used to say, "I'll murder you if you don't . . ." Is all that is necessary in therapy for a patient to find someone who can stand it a little better, someone who says murder is real but not everything? Yes, we kill each other and see each other tomorrow or next week to do it again and maybe talk of it, feel it, and feel other things as well. Moments of beauty escape murder. But more, at last Burt says that he feels moments of beauty before murder swallows them. And these moments are real too. But we must not make much of it.

———————

Murder of true self, murder as true self. What is this bush burning in indestructible innocence as murder incessantly consumes it? Innocence and experience.

Nothing is more true for Burt than murder, nothing more false. Because something is being murdered, something most precious of all—life, truth, soul, love, caring, compassion, kindness, sensitivity, relationship. What is left is a murderous force with nothing but murder, nothing left to murder—it has all been swept away. Yet Burt cannot stop being spokesman for what is murdered. He grinds his truth into the ground and is frustrated beyond endurance that what he feels does not change the world. His soul screaming from the most secret places does not make life kinder, gentler. He works to make himself a better person but most of the time feels he failed. He cannot, dare not stop. He believes if only we know, it will be different. Evidence for this belief remains scanty.

Moments of beauty escape murder. Thus there is some evidence for miracles. Something happens sometimes. Is that enough? All there can be? For Burt that is an argument for life as a form of suicide, literal suicide preferable. What keeps him alive? What drives him to keep trying? What makes it impossible to stop as long as breath moves him? What deeper ethics makes his flesh say that soul counts, must count, for everyone?

## SNAKE BITE

Jack is in the clear. His life came together. Loving relationship with his wife in a sexless marriage, raising family, nucleus of everyday life. Fulfilling sex with a caring mistress, support for nucleus, life's overflowing cup. Creative work, making CD's with artists he believes in. He worked hard getting to this place. For a long time, he feared he would have to give something up to make a go of it. But good work, family, eros all became possible, not the way he imagined when he was younger, not all together, at once, but separately, a modular life.

Then he dreamt of a poisonous snake biting him, bringing back childhood terrors.

Were things going too well? Something bad had to happen? How much goodness can one take? The snake as fear of punishment, punishment itself? Reversal of affect (good to bad), turning against the self? A snake in the garden of one's soul.

Snake as sense of truth, giving the lie to ways we poison ourselves by what we covet, by how we use or misuse our lives?

Jack is in conflict about deserving or not deserving goodness. "I have and don't have the right to good things." Goodness translates into good things, and good things purvey goodness. To some extent, snake is spoiler. "I spoil good things that happen, but refuse to let my spoiler win." For some, the fight against the tendency to spoil life is a fight to the death. But there really is goodness and spoiling, and goodness survives spoiling, and spoiling survives goodness.

———

Law of the Dream: No amount of goodness will silence or end the work of the biting, poisonous snake. To be without this snake is to be without truth. It is not just that we are angry or sad about the snake spoiling paradise, or that we give in to temptation. If we omit the snake from the garden of soul, we are less than truthful.

Truth bites like a snake and poisons the well-being that adaptations bring. Truth is rarely toothless or without sting, and we fight it like a poison spoiling the good we have achieved.

Yet snake is also ego, the dream a critique of ego, a critique of how we injure ourselves by the way we live. We injure ourselves by the good we seek and how we seek it. Jack poisons his soul by the success of his own personality.

Jack wanted family, eros, creative work. Life frustrated him, but he rose to the challenge. He refused to give up on himself and kept to his wishes and goals. Through good fortune and hard work he found ways to piece together areas of being that he desired. No doubt he would have been worse had he failed. Why call an ego refusing defeat snaky? This places Jack in the position of poisoning himself if he succeeds or fails.

Indeed, this may be part of the hard fact the dream imparts. There is no way to avoid a snakeless life, a life free of self-poisoning processes. There is something stark and simple about the truth of the snake, something one can't con away.

There were times Jack felt that he tricked his way through life, that in merely being alive he got away with something. With a poisonous snake biting one's soul, just being alive is miraculous. Yet Jack felt more. Goodness surviving poison is a gift indeed.

---

The snake in the garden takes many turns. People call it sensation, pride, sin, evil, impulse, ego, genitals, hyperconsciousness, cunning, wisdom. A sense of something bad changes forms, and sometimes we try to get rid of it, tear out or dissolve the bad thing, the spoiler. Sometimes we try to broaden our attitude, to make room for it, observe its transformations, get to know its twists and turns.

Can one snake the snake away?

Snake mind, dove heart.

The flesh as enemy of spirit is a viewpoint that has moments. But more important is the spirit itself. It is not simply a matter of lower-higher, but the quality and tone of how we approach ourselves. An evil mind wreaks more havoc than weakness of flesh. Good and evil spirit, not simply flesh and spirit or drive and ego. What sort of drive? What sort of ego? How do we taste to ourselves?

Jack tries to tell himself he tastes good, life tastes good. Indeed, this is so. But the poisonous bite does not vanish. The good he holds cannot obliterate the conscience of his dreams. Dream conscience is terrifying. It threatens to be uncontrollable.

Snake spirit tortures him.

Some people bitten by dream conscience never recover. They spend their lives working with the poison, aware how evil they are. They wrestle with themselves, ever in danger of succumbing to evil impulse and spirit. They know they are dangerous to themselves and others and can't look away for a moment.

Jack does not seem in danger of vanishing in the sense of evil. He resists the evil vision or circumscribes it. Life feels too good to him to give in totally to the snake within. He makes things a little bit easy on himself, although he is committed to living fully. He does not seem to have a place in his self-image for the poisonous snake. It does not fit his picture of himself. He is so convincing in toning down the snake bite of the dream that he makes me wonder about my severity.

Do dreams lie?

I am everything in my dreams. The poisoned and the poisonous, the bitten and the biting, maligned-malignant, the wound that never heals and the one who wounds.

I am my dream. My dream is me.

I am a poisonous snake that bites myself.

My dream is a poisonous snake telling me my view of self leaves something to be desired. I have not come to the bottom of whatever I am. Snake bite takes me into mystery.

We may never exhaust our sense of what the eternal snake bite tries to tell us. And we will not rid ourselves of the bite by analyzing it.

The biting snake cannot be wished away, made to disappear by understanding, or vanquished by struggle. We return to it, it to us; it never leaves. As Blake says, all states, perhaps tendencies, are eternal.

For Jack, the biting snake is "out there," other, mystery. He is not wrong. Dreams are multidirectional, pointing out and in. For Jack, the not-me element of the snake presides over the me-ness element. The snake is not embraced as part of self so much as located outside self as threat, as trauma.

Jack was terrified of snakes in childhood, but more terrifying still were dream snakes. In actual life no snake harmed him. But the chance was there that one might. He was harmed more by people, but his terror landed on snakes. As a child, he could not find the thought that mental snakes were a source of terror, although even then he knew he was terrified and fascinated by his mind.

Snake as a symbol of mind, mindsnakes. Poisonous mind, breathtaking mind, hard-working mind, imaginative mind.

Snake journeys. I am and am not my snakemind.

"Get away from me," a first reaction.

"Look at that, what is it? Let me put it in my mouth, taste it deep inside me." Another first reaction.

For Jack, snake was potential trauma, injury, partly symbolic of parental trauma. Danger out there, real.

And the trauma of being alive? Where is that located?

Lifesnake, kundalini energy, chi, Tao, Zen. One can know life to death but it slides away, hides, finds another day. Jack came out on the lucky side, more pleasure than pain.

Early dreamsnake terrors subsided when Jack became a young man. Childhood terrors express fear of experience. When Jack jumped into youthful experience, early fears diminished. The meaning of snake as genital refers to dread of experience. Movement between innocence and experience goes along with movement between dread and despair.

Genital and mind and spirit. Child and parent. Object and self. Energy and shifting centers. Tree of Knowledge, Tree of Life. Mind-snake, lifesnake, snake power. The snake of meaning. Rebirth—renewal—shedding skin. Snake runs through them.

Jack had much pleasure with his snake sexually, mentally, spiritually, yet it appears in his dream as enemy. Yet if one looks closely at snakes of his childhood dreams, they have a healthy look and like to sun themselves. Only in adulthood does a poisonous dream-snake bite him. The bite of therapy. The bite of the mind one tries to escape, the mind one never can quite discover, restless snake-mind. It takes years to build up to undergoing the bite of life, the full poison. It would annihilate a young soul.

Jack was more entranced by experience than afraid of it. He did not let fear of life stop him from living it. An unconscious solution was to parcel out domains, separating eros from family and work, making all more manageable. A fairly old-fashioned solution at that.

Return of the snake merely as a momentary terror in the night. Jack tries out ways to tone the snake down, but he is growing interested. Is the time coming when he can attend a little longer, a little closer, glimpsing the snake breathing through him?

A good life does not dissolve the rage of the snake.

Snake rage.

Meanings do not slake its thirst.

here are mischievous and malignant rages. In psychosis the two combine in ways that baffle, repulse, and fascinate. Is it odd to say there is something mischievous in madness? Usually, fusion of dread and rage in madness seems humorless. More than life and self is at stake. One's being is blasted with corrosive, malignant flare-ups of affective thoughts and visions that make limitless hell present now. What is worse than present hell is a foreboding certainty of ever worsening hells to come. One is sealed in black promises of everything horrifying one hoped to escape, no letup in sight.

Yet there is mischievousness in madness. Sly, cunning—popular portrayals of madness key into it. It is as if the madman is fascinated with his own madness. Some part is out of the storm, not just as observer or witness, but as sick comedian. As a spy.

There is mischievous, malignant rage.

In a short passage, Bion brings together digestion, sex, and birth, which have deep symbolic connections. What is at issue is digesting experience, which involves many kinds of intercourse (with our own and others' experience), and birthing new or further experience. In a way, digestion leads to birth and is part of birth, and birth is part of digestion—when it comes to feelings and ideas.

In psychosis, psychic digestion is damaged. This may be the case for everyone, more or less. Bion points to madness as especially illuminating in studying digestive failure, deformation, skew. Perhaps this is because in madness a disaster has happened to personality, and attempts to process (digest) disaster become personality's obsession, the latter tending to compound rather than "solve" catastrophe.

Sometimes the distinction between mental and physical digestion is not great, either mistaken for the other, the two mixed up. In Bion's example, X, his patient (actual, generic?) gets into a mental state in which he spies on his mother's insides, her digestive-reproductive processes. Digestion-sex-reproduction amalgamate, and the patient becomes hypersensitive to a fusion of imaginary/ real sound. Clicking, banging—sexual and digestive sounds are amplified, at once physical and mental, the individual persecuted by his auditory capacity, engorged by fantasy.

The result of this digestion-birth process is not to create a person, but a stool. X tries to spy on something degrading, a spoiling process, his own dehumanization. He is a kind of a reverse alchemist, documenting the turning of soul gold to shit, birthing a familiar monster, the outcome of a sick or aborted digestive process. Mental digestion leads to birth through intercourse with life. X points to something going wrong, something *always* going wrong, something wrong with life.

Life as digestion-birth doesn't work right. X gets banged and chewed to bits, a corrosive, fragmenting process, in which generativity seems turned against itself. He is looking for someone's insides to digest him. We take in what is good for us, things that taste good. We digest each other. But X no longer has faith in such a possibility, although he can't stop hoping altogether. In a malignant and persistent way, he spies on bad insides, hoping for something better, or at least to see things as they are.

He spies on someone's insides turning him to shit, as he is unable to generate a sound digestive process of his own. One partly does to others what was partly done to oneself. X is unable to digest another human being in a good way and persists in reliving, or, rather, getting a view on (control of?), a disaster that has befallen the capacity to be human.

One fights for real psychic digestive-birthing ability but is stuck mocking the latter's undoing. This stuck mocking has a sickly comedic aspect, hoping to blast through itself, yet at the same time dancing above the explosions. Digestive, sexual, birthing explosions—in which the possibility of digestion, intercourse, and birth keep blowing themselves up. Malignant and inane laughter limes corrosive and explosive processes. One mocks one's own disintegration. So-called hebephrenic silliness and sly, idiotic laughter reflect the sense that blowing oneself up, blowing life up, is a big joke.

X tries to get into his mother's insides, his analyst's insides. Is he trying to find his own insides by proxy or escape them? One substitutes another's insides for one's own. If Lacan is right, there are ways in which the other's insides *are* one's own. We grow inside the desire of the other as in a petri dish. We answer to or evade the fact of mutual permeability and attempt to control, at least limit, self spreading through self. We may pretend we are not interwoven, running like color stains through one another, and even kill to prove the point, but murder, above all, is a testament to fusion.

Bion imagines that X's desire to get deeply into him is akin to parental intercourse seen as digestion of one parent by the other. It is a digestion to be envied, especially if it works. If only parents could or would digest each other—if only *someone's* psychical digestion worked. Unfortunately, digestion here probably means indigestion. Perhaps X is stuck with the fact that his parents gave each other mental indigestion. And that he was inserted into a world where insides never had digestive possibilities. Is X bent on proving that digestion exists or doesn't exist?

What is he looking for inside the analyst, the mother? Is he looking for a father? Is he trying to prove that insides are different or the same? That his are just like everyone else's? My sense is that a monster is looking and being looked for through the sense of the body and feel of the mind. Something monstrous happened to the possibility of being human, and X is glued to it—he must see it and pin it down, although the weird thing is he probably sees nothing else.

Is it only a matter of undoing difference? The Ten Commandments tried to erect barriers against attacks on difference. Don't envy your neighbor's goods or wife, don't kill, commit adultery, or take what's not yours. Respect generations, honor parents (children too, one hopes?). Love God, not idols, and work on respecting boundaries. X doesn't seem to care much about boundaries. He might argue legalistically, "Anyway, those are external boundaries. I trespass invisible ones." X wants to see *everything,* although one senses a toxic everything. A mental eye exercises invasive rights, peremptory usurpation of another's inner privacy, incessant psychic endoscopy-colonoscopy. Perhaps, if he could, X would be invisible and steal through the other's psychic bloodstream, satisfying himself that nothing was worth having, driven by the sense that everything must be had. Is this, partly, a way of annihilating the sense that something essential is missing by scientifically proving that, anyway, it is no good and may not even exist?

Entering and controlling the other has mental and physical aspects. One wants to control the other's mind, the other's desire. One wants to control the other's body. In outright madness, mind control may be most important. In political and erotic power, the latter may be prominent. Of course, these are not mutually exclusive domains, and they permeate each other. One seeks both to damage and repair, to repair and damage, hope against hope, despair against despair.

Fantasies of controlling physical insides limit the spread of mental powers. X marks out digestion and reproduction as his battlefield, providing focus to circumscribe the spread of dread. Without such physical concerns, the battlefield would be unmarked, unlocalized. There is a dimension of psychosis in which dread of mental influence is boundless. The idea of bodies (inside or outside) loses power as a limit and dread of malign spirits escalates. Immaterial spirit or mind instantaneously can be anywhere, everywhere. Everything is in danger of being exposed. At least spying on someone's digestive-reproductive processes takes some degree of work. When it comes to the body, even omnipotence takes time.

Moses sent spies to report on the land of promise, the holy land. The spies came back and said the land is filled with giants — milk and honey, yes, but too frightening. The Hebrews in the wilderness would be like grasshoppers, they said. The spies were punished for being demoralizing (being demoralizing is already a pun-ishment) and faithful Joshua led the way, so the drama continued to unfold. Is X a demoralized-demoralizing spy? Is the Moses-Joshua line missing or hidden in Bion's story of X? X's spying is parasitic. The promised land is mother-analyst's insides melded with parental intercourse. X can neither truly enjoy what he sees, make use of digestive-generative capacities, nor tear himself away. He is mesmerized by what he wishes he could be and use, but re-mains in disdainful dread of. The land of plenty is someone else. He can sneak a look and merely watch it all go bad—a kind of re-verse Midas, as if seeing spoils what is seen.

The spy is some kind of body ego fragment broken off and watching itself, a bit of mental stool turned into a sliver of observ-ing consciousness. Can anything good survive its glance? Is the end of digestive parental intercourse orgasm, fertility, the possi-bility of engendering life, or confirmation that anything can be fe-calized? Is X looking for a conclusion that escapes the evil eye or a pat on the backside reassuring him that everything stinks? There is rage if something good survives and rage if it doesn't. Spying is a form of lustful rage imagining what one spies on longs to sur-render but never will. The spy is confused and further frustrated if his quarry eludes fecalization by refusing fusion with the demoral-izing viewpoint.

Bion says X must watch to the bitter end, and in so doing "loses touch with his *base.*" This is what the "commandments" warn against and why there is particular issue with heart following eyes. As mothers used to say, "Your eyes are bigger than your stomach." Digestion can't keep up with all the good things to eat and is even in worse shape if compelled to digest a proliferation of bad things.

Comparison shopping, keeping an eye on one's neighbor, has its benefits. Among its dangers is diffusion of self, loss of touch with one's base. In the Bible, one's base is God, in Bion's terms (loosely speaking), O (at-onement). But what if one's O, one's very sense of aliveness, is off—poisoned, warped, traumatized, malformed?

X seems to be in this predicament. He tries to right life by spying on it, going into others, deeper and deeper, as if by seeing or tasting one more thing, he will find what he seeks. Instead, he heads toward the bitter end, seeing more and more of the same unsatisfactory thing, changing only the speed of rushing. And if there is a bitter end, what will it be?

To be glued to another's digestive, generative processes is to lose one's own, unless one is trying to jump start one's own by taking in another's, using the other as stimulus, seeing how another does it, or somehow by resonance getting one's own to work. X, however, is in danger of losing more of himself the more he eyes the other. Yet I feel something noble in X's pursuit of another's base, at the expense of his own. It is as if he is affirming something valuable somewhere, something he wants, something he keeps trying to get. He does not give up easily. He is very persistent in his attempt to visually exploit or apprehend another's insides in lieu of his own — even if he must spoil them, or even if they are spoiled. It is as if he is saying insides are real and important and somewhere they must do their job, if only I can locate a place that works, a moment of value.

Am I being too optimistic? Isn't there anything about Bion that works? Is there nothing in the therapy couple that enables growth? We pass through each other's digestive systems like soil through worms, fertilizing cultural worlds that support us more than air does. We are lucky if we make the best of a bad job. But there are X's riveted to bad digestion, partly hoping for better, partly turning better into worse. The X Bion describes is attached (addicted) to a kind of visual version of smelling feces and farts, watching what others do with psychic material destined to be lost. We keep trying to see how we are damaged, how damage occurs.

Perhaps we posit or hope for or actually sense some small x which escapes damage or does not add to it, or, at least, wants to and can learn something about working with it. Dare we have faith that something may come of the couple, X and Bion, even though the couple itself is absorbed in a prolonged disaster, O, which binds them together? Instruments of psychoanalytic work —mind or psychic being—cannot escape the influence of forces worked with. One is altered by what one tries to alter, changed by what one tries to change.

The pursuit of depth as a means of salvation: X cannot pierce the secret. Not only because depth is endless, or because X's seeing spoils what is seen (or is spoiled by it). Surface too is endless, easily assaulted and spoiled. Depth may be used to defend against surface, as surface defends against depth (often, too, each defends the other). Neither escapes the work of damaging processes. Either may be sought for refuge. Each possesses infinities, and the mind that works them is capable of further thinking/imagining. It is not X's fault if he fails to get to the bitter end. But there is something of the scientist in his attempt to keep seeing, to go as far as he can, and keep going.

Has he mistaken mind for body, body for mind? Does he intuit their dense connection, oneness? By going deeper and deeper, mystics discover a soul point pure and incorruptible opening to God. But this soul point can remain unconscious and the God-pop may take the form of luminous world, as when the night sky (in one story) opened Buddha's mind. Can X get there through digestive insides, fantasy travel through another's organs? If he does, will the God-pop be spoiled by his method of achievement, or will he burst into another form of existence?

Rage can spoil or purify.

X tries to get deeply into mother's insides, parental intercourse, analyst's mind. I think X tries to go both or all ways at once: more deeply into and away from life, directions possibly no longer distinguishable from one another. And what would more life mean? Bion writes, " 'Deeply' here means multi-dimensionally extreme— in space, in time, in 'thoroughness,' in emotional involvement."

There is good depth and bad depth or ways of going deeply or relating to depth. If there is enough free unconscious flow, the two spiral, reverse, mix, and support personal growth. Experience opens up. One is led to new pastures through the valley of death. There are those of us who cannot live without depth, including rubbing and banging against extremes, limits, edges of our psychic universe. One attempts to push past what it is possible to experience.

One can drive a sports car as fast as it can go and get the thrill of the edge of the possible. It is not certain that personality evolves from this, but it may. An activity like this, repeated over and over, is more like standing in one place. Life may move on, interests change, one may see others die in crashes. There is something of this thrill and compulsion revving psychic motors, breaking through personal walls. The gain is resonance, subtle shifts in the ways one vibes, a growing need to pay attention to life's touch, the feel of things, and the feel of the feel of things.

Rage explodes walls, becomes a wall itself. As experience opens, attention turns to the rage coursing through it, part of the feel of life, the strength of life, God's might. One is never less than fury, but also much more. X's fury is trapped in fantasies of organs. His wish is for insides that move life on. His method is like a sports car headed nowhere, dissolving the world into pure speed, inner eyes a high-speed engine, outracing time, turning space inside out.

The mind of the analyst, rage and all, becomes a place where touch is possible, a place accommodating, outlasting obliteration, where self says for moments, "My God, I am here." A here—a hearing—that lets obliteration be. X is assaulted by hearing. The sound of his own heart is a death chamber. The analyst's voice, connected to heart-mind, says, yes, all this is real.

PINCHAS

Rage cleans the stain of sin.
Righteous wrath cleans the state, the soul, the cosmos.
Moral rage.
Pinchas's burning rage sets things right.
Something is rotten in the state. Hamlet must kill to right things.

Something is wrong with Israel, whoring with other Gods (again). Murder rights things.

The story begins at the end of *Balak,* in the *Book of Numbers,* 25:1–9, and extends to *Pinchas* in *Numbers,* 25:10 to 30:1. In Hebrew it is customary to call this fourth Book of Moses *Bamidbar,* "In the Wilderness," loosely taken from the fourth word of the first sentence of the book. God speaks to Moses in the tent of meeting in the wilderness of Sinai, telling him to take a census of males over the age of twenty who can go to war.

Commentators tell us God delights in counting the Israelites, like a rich man takes pleasure in counting his fortune, wondrous jewels readying to march on Canaan as God's war machine. A link between counting and violence. To count is to count those who can kill. Fighting men are precious to a community bent on conquest. Killers for the community count.

Part of the story: Hebrew men began bonding with Moabite women, which led to bonding with "the Baal of Peor," local gods. God got mad (rage kindled like fire) and told Moses to hang all the Israeli chiefs. Moses went to the judges and told them to kill the men who bonded with Baal-Peor. At this moment of lament and purification, a man brought a local woman to the gathering "in the sight of Moses, and in the sight of all the congregations of the children of Israel, while they were weeping at the door of the tent

(124)

of meeting." This was more than Pinchas, son of Eliezar, son of Aharon the priest (Moses' brother), could bear. He killed the man and woman with his spear, through her belly, arresting the plague consuming Israel at twenty-four thousand victims.

Death cleanses—murder cleanses. Illness cleanses.

Soul is pure. Life soils. Purification measures must be taken. Death wipes the slate clean.

In the beginning of the next section, *Pinchas,* God's purification prescription continues. God tells Moses that Pinchas's jealousy for Him has turned His jealous rage from Israel. He gives Pinchas His covenant of *shalom* (peace!) and the covenant of everlasting priesthood, perpetuating the priestly line from Aharon through Eliezar, Pinchas, and the latter's descendents—"because he was jealous for his God and made atonement for the children of Israel."

The murdered couple is identified. The man is Zimri, a prince from the tribe of Shimon, a line that has had its hotheads. The woman, Cozbi, was daughter of a Midianite chief. To flaunt their union at such a moment must have been a kind of protest, an expression of freedom. It flew in the face of Israelites weeping over their betrayal of God and the punishment at hand. Just as Israel is refinding God, this couple comes and laughs at them. God tells Moses to harass and kill the Midianites, "for they harass you by their wiles, beguiling you through women, like Cozbi, turning you away."

It is not until the section, *Mattos,* that the bloody business of killing Midianites begins. The rest of *Pinchas* deals with census taking, laws, and sacrifices, as if the return to God necessitates recommitment, review, amplification. Extension of godly law begins by granting women more legal rights, particularly inheritance rights, perhaps a reward for demonstrating greater fidelity than men, contrasting faithful Israeli women with deceptive Midianites, who lure men to their gods through their bodies.

Moses has the people's attention, having killed the faithless. Those remaining after the plague and the slaughter are numbered, told laws anew, enter into serious discussions about legal rights and sacrificial duties. A kind of purification occurs. God through Moses sets things straight, catalyzed by Pinchas's righteous zeal. *Then* the fighting begins.

After further discussion of vows, God tells Moses to arm a thousand men from each tribe and attack. Pinchas went too, as a priest, holding "the holy vessels and the trumpets." They killed every Midianite male, the five Midianite kings, and Bilam the prophet or soothsayer. They brought back women and spoils (flocks, goods), and Moses said angrily, "You saved the women who caused this trouble through Bilam's advice, the same who caused children of Israel to break faith with the Lord in the matter of Peor, igniting the plague?" Moses ordered the male children killed and only allowed virginal women to remain alive for the soldiers.

We must recognize links between violence and cleansing. Hitler purified the Jewish blot by murder. Hebrews sought to purify themselves by cutting out idolaters within and polluters without.

Still, the situation is more complicated than it looks. Moses' wife was the daughter of Jethro, a Midianite sage who sheltered Moses and later set up the latter's judicial system. Mosaic lines hinged on fidelity to God, not just tribal allegiance—up to a point. It is difficult to tease out military, nationalistic, and religious threads. How much was the Mosaic calculus (rage with a reason) bent on warding off assimilation, so as not to thin the budding, yet-to-be nation? Moses did not want his fighters to become part of the groups they had to beat.

It is said that Moses planned to travel around the Midianites, not attack them, partly because of past ties. However, Balak, a Midianite chieftain, was edgy. He saw the Hebrews camping nearby, feared assault, and prepared to strike first. He asked Bilam (magician, sage, priest, prophet?) to bless his cause and curse the Hebrews, but each time Bilam tried to do so, he did the opposite. He could say only good about the Hebrews, so much so that his words are the first said today upon entering the synagogue.

Apparently Balak deferred attack and instead followed Bilam's advice to neutralize Israel covertly, through contact with Midianite women. The plague of assimilation threatened until Pinchas throttled it. The brazenness of Zimri and Cozbi brought things to a symbolic head, and Pinchas pricked the bubble.

The whole thing might have been averted had Balak not followed Bilam's advice or if Bilam had not given in to Balak's fear and hatred. The great IF—such is the rationalization for the biblical slaughter of the Midianites. Of course, the Israelites who succumbed to idolatry were killed too.

There is something clean about Pinchas's rage—clean rage—pure rage, pure and purifying, like Flannery O'Connor's destroyers, cleaning the spiritual body, the body of the faithful. "Rintrah roars and shakes his fiery head from side to side," writes Blake. Blake's devils, fiery, alive, irrepressible energic bursts, revolutionary. What a spectrum rage spans—from Pinchas the enforcer to the high-voltage Blakean devil, throbbing with affective intensity and imaginative heat.

Rebel-establishment. Rage runs through it.

The Hebrew revolt against the Egyptians. The Hebrew establishment, Moses, priests, judges—God's law the center. Binding former slaves together. Binding tribes. Law as cement. God's voice runs through the nation's veins.

God's face is the heart center.

The Law is alive with godly energy and as Blake says, "Energy is Eternal Delight."

The father unites desire and law (according to Lacan). There is desire-law fusion until vision fades. Symbolic father, Name of the Father. Letter killeth, spirit giveth life.

There is a Pinchas inside aimed at bullshit.

If we look at circuits of meaning, we find crosscurrents, reversibility, splitting, fusion, layering, piling on, spinning off . . .

Pinchas is on the side of the godly establishment. God is Moses' steadfast organizational and personal center. Laws bind the nation together—but they are God's laws. They are vehicles of relationship with God. There is a personal relationship at the center of law. God and Moses meet, speak, hear and see each other—mystical vision at the heart of godly law, momentous godly reality seen, heard, felt with one's whole being. There is whole-being perception, whole-being experiencing. Every node of conscious/unconscious being hears and sees and feels God. Every Jew through all time shares this common center, this whole-being experiencing of God.

The Bible is about betrayal and return. The basic heart-mind-soul vision, and the law that grows out of it, is repeatedly betrayed. Whoring after other gods, the great crime involving soul collapse, lack of faith, associated with demoralization, fear, and being misled by what seems attractive to one's own eyes and heart. Betrayal of God associated with betrayal of heart. Diotima tells Socrates how the soul progresses up the ladder of the Good, from good to good, until it reaches its true anchor and liberation, goodness itself. Along the way, wild or ignorant or evil horses are tamed, educated, brought in line with the program. There is something in the self that is resistant to education even while craving it. It may be that the black horse is never fully tamed or brought into line. We need its resistance as part of something larger. Moses tries to tame the wild horses of Israel, bind them to the greater body, and, at times, if necessary, kill them. As the Bible ends, we do not know what the outcome will be. The drama goes on between spirit of wisdom-faith and countertendencies. There is, too, individuality, Blake's devil, spokesperson for energy and self that never gives in, refusal of systems. The God who leads us out of one system yokes us to another—at once revolution and establishment, oneness of desire-law.

### Countertendencies:
### Bilam, Balak, Korach, Spies, Sophists

Balak, a Moabite leader, feared the gathering of Hebrews near his land and asked the prophet Bilam to curse them. God told Bilam the Hebrews were blessed, not cursed, but Bilam gives in to baser inclinations and Balak's emissaries. Instead of refusing to go with them, he waits to see if God will change His mind. A more purely righteous person might not hem and haw and look for an out. But Bilam does what many of us might—procrastinate and hope things take another turn.

He is, perhaps, afraid for his skin and desirous of reward, and he bows to simple pressures to get God to give in a little. But the moment of truth is merely postponed.

It is noteworthy that Balak, whose people worship other gods (Baal of Peor), believes in Jahveh's power and feels strongly that Bilam is an avenue of access to the latter. "If you curse them, they are cursed; if not, not," says Balak, hoping for God's blessing. It is to Balak's credit that he did not kill Bilam. He recognized a greater force was working. He would not harm a prophet.

Bilam, as avenue of access to God's will, has no personal interest in the outcome. God's will is God's will. A prophet must mold himself in light of this. However, there is more to Bilam than God's point of access. He is a man with mixed urges, needs, weaknesses, wishes. Zen writings speak of practiced students, even masters, losing their Zen before a king. Why does Bilam, like Esau, get harsh treatment by the rabbis?

There is a biblical thread of figures regarded as linked with evil or lesser tendencies, following Cain, Ham, Esau. Bilam is a variation. Esau is more body ego, Bilam more mental ego, devious. It was he who advised Balak to get the Hebrews to bring God's curse upon themselves by idolatry, to bring down Israeli Zimris via Midianite Cozbis. Such subversive cleverness in the face of God made rabbis curse Bilam.

Can one blame Bilam? He was playing by the rules. But—true enough—he was manipulating rules to subvert the Name of the Father, playing on God's rage, God's weakness. Jacob was sneaky but somehow his cleverness linked with the soul's love of God. Bilam's actions tainted that love. David sinned and repented. One cannot conceive of David without love of God, whatever his failings. One does not feel this wholehearted passion with Bilam. The latter tries to trick God by manipulating the psychospiritual dimension of life. His trickery is not meant to bring hearts closer to

God's heart. One does not hear of repentance, even when his plan, successful to a point, ultimately fails and he dies as a result of his scheme (apparently killed by Pinchas's forces).

Bilam links with sophists, who can argue any point of view convincingly. Socrates, in Plato's dialogue *Sophist,* is a kind of mental Pinchas, more intricate and interesting, attempting to show that sophistry has fatal flaws. If one cannot hold truth in one's hand, neither can one nullify it with chains of signifiers, no matter how subtle. Socrates' sword is a good heart, faith, pursuit of wisdom, relentless questioning. Irony is a tool, not the last word. In Plato's *Phaedo,* Socrates does not try to escape the verdict of the state, let alone God's. Yet his acquiescence to the death sentence imposed on him stands as one of the greatest critiques of sophistic abuse of power in cultural history. He is the manifestation of a truth drive in human life, truth hunger, love of wisdom, good faith. His sword goes through the heart of rhetorical skill alone, verbal samurai for hire.

The Bible often has violent "solutions" to problems — solutions that don't really solve. Korach voices doubts of the people or some of the Hebrew elite: "Who do you think you are, Moses? All of us are holy. Why do you put yourself above us?" Moses falls to the ground, demonstrating he is God's servant, not high above. He is furious and asks, rather tells, God to consume the rebels. God is enraged and wants to destroy the whole population (as usual), but Moses talks him into targeting the biggest troublemakers.

One might be cynical and ask, if God killed all of them, who would be left for Moses to lead? We hear Moses muttering about fairness: he has not taken anything from anyone for his trouble, "not one ass, neither have I hurt one of them." No taint of self-interest motivates his work. Tests are devised to tell the true from the false, so "you'll know God sent me to do all these works, and that I have not done them of mine own mind."

Rabbis are harsh with Korach, as with Bilam, Esau, and Ham. He represents envy, a turn of mind drawing on holiness twisted by invidious comparison (echoing back to beginnings, Cain and

Abel, Adam-Eve's envious desire of more or other). The serpent as hero, transforming into Satan, adversary, accuser, spoiler, forcing individuation, through loss, trials, tragedy, death. Korach and Pinchas, dualities in the soul—or is Korach not substantive enough?

Always a twist. Korach, voice of democracy. "We are all holy. We all should have a say, an equal say, a say as good as yours, Moses. You take too much on yourself, you put yourself too high. One person, one vote. At least, fairer representation." Korach was voice for 250 men, "princes of the congregation, elect men of the assembly, men of renown."

Moses cut through his democratic rhetoric. Korach is from the tribe of Levi, which God privileged to perform rituals and minister to the people. "This is not enough for you?" asks Moses. "You want to displace Aharon?" Moses exposes Korach's jealous ambition, democratic pretense in pursuit of power. Here is subtle kinship with Bilam (several chapters ahead) and the spies (two chapters earlier): dissimulation to undermine spirit, create paralyzing doubt, reverse the terms of faith. Using God's name to warp or betray the godly bond takes God's name in vain in a deeper sense than swearing oaths.

Levites were the faithful in the matter of the golden calf. How could Aharon, who succumbed, be placed above them? Does kinship take precedence over faith? Shouldn't the golden calf nullify Aharon's heart of gold? Who is higher, who is lower, who has more, who has less? It galled Korach that Aharon might have greater merit than he. Are the roots of true democracy in Mosaic law or Korach's temperament? Korachs of the world turn democracy and law into what suits them at the moment. Democracy collapses into veiled lust for power. Unfairness runs through the Bible. But would Abel have killed Cain if the situation had been reversed? Nevertheless, God kills Korach, setting the stage for Pinchas's godly rage.

Korach and the Levite princes were not alone. Dathan and Abiram and their men, from the tribe of Reuben, joined him. Dathan and Abiram did not share Korach's priestly aspirations but argued that Moses failed to fulfill his promise: "You took us out of a land flowing with milk and honey and have not brought us to a land flowing with milk and honey, nor given us inheritance of fields and vineyards. From you flows nothing but hardship with no reward." A revolt is brewing, a call for change of power and direction, whether a return to Egypt or settling down and making a go of it. What reason does Moses have to imagine God wouldn't be on the side of the revolt, given the impoverished life belonging to his leadership?

Moses sets up a series of tests in which God must choose between Aharon and Korach and his allies, which Aharon wins. This results in a hole opening in the earth beneath the rebels, into which they vanish. Legend has it that if you put your ear next to the crack that remains on the spot, you can hear Korach and his men crying, "Moses and the Torah are true, we are liars." All Hebrews may be holy, but there is holy and holy. Terror of the ground opening beneath one expresses a primordial agony coming not only from outside but inside the self. The practical result was the consolidation of the priesthood by Aharon and his descendents, immediately Eliezar and then Pinchas. The Levites were ritual helpers.

After each violent end to a challenge of Mosaic authority, God gave Moses more laws for the people. Violence got their attention and, for a time, made them more responsive. After the priesthood was firmly established, Aharon could die. With military, judicial, and priesthood groupings in order, Moses would soon pass on too. Already the budding nation, organized by God's laws, was nipping towns of Canaan. Soon only two of the original men who left Egypt, Joshua and Caleb, would be alive, and the mantle of leadership would pass to Joshua. But first—as always—more trials.

One reason Pinchas's violence was tolerated—extolled—was because it affirmed the power of the priesthood. Now, with Aharon gone and Eliezar an old man, Pinchas demonstrated that the priestly line had punch. A thread of uncompromised integrity and resolve opposed forces of assimilation and the collapse of Mosaic authority. A stroke of the sword reestablished the power of faith. Integrity lives, the message. A great biblical trope is Israel's wedding to God, jealous lover. God must be the one and only. Israel must have a monogamous relationship with God. God has a monogamous relationship with everyone. Here God is Freud's leader of the primal horde. But God tries to establish just principles for all to live by, flowing from prohibition against deicide.

The story of the spies is several chapters before Korach and forms an associative link with the latter. God tells Moses to choose esteemed men from each tribe to spy on Canaan and prepare for attack. Some students feel that the Hebrews just scored a stunning victory in southern Canaan (Hormah) and could have gone on to take the land then and there. Perhaps frightened by their own success and beset by a faint-hearted streak, they held back and asked to see what they were up against. Thus *Shelach Lecha,* the title of this section, could mean, "You want to take a look, so go ahead, send spies!" Like God telling Bilam, "You want to do what you want, so go to Balak!" Where Bilam could not take no for an answer, the Israelites here could not take yes.

The majority of spies came back with disheartening reports. "The land eats up its inhabitants and the men are giants. We were as grasshoppers in our own sight and in theirs." The people are dismayed and want to go back to Egypt. It is hard to tell if they are being hysterical or really mean it. But they certainly express discontent, possible demoralization, and unease with Moses' leadership. Of the spies, only Caleb and Joshua remain firm. "It is an exceedingly good land," they say. "If God delights in us, we will win. Don't rebel against God. The Lord is with us and they [the Canaanites] are bread." Tumult follows. The people balk. God gets mad and wants to destroy them all. Moses once again talks him out of it. But all the people who came out of Egypt, with the exception of Caleb and Joshua, will die wandering in the desert another thirty-eight years. Those who fight with Joshua will never have known Egypt, have nowhere to go back to, and, presumably, won't hold back.

This story never ends. The drama of doubt and faith takes endless twists and turns. Not only the people and the heads of tribes, but also Moses' own sister, faults him. One way or another, God afflicts Moses' enemies, even in his own family. The story spans and links personal/mystical and political levels, fusing the two. God scolds Miriam and Aharon, reminding them that He appears to prophets in visions but speaks to Moses mouth to mouth. God says Moses is uniquely humble, unlike other men. In Moses' case, meekness and rage go together. While Moses has made more of a clearing for God than most, self-nullification isn't complete. Moses' rage passes on to Pinchas's sword, while his wisdom settles on Joshua.

A lot of work goes into dealing with rage, Moses', God's, Pinchas's. Freud's writings on Michelangelo's statue of Moses emphasize relentless tension between rage and self-restraint, fury and mastery. What does one do with rage? When to hold it back, when to let it out, how to direct it? Does containing it build psychic muscles? Raging is an important way to feel one's body, to feel alive. In the Bible, rage can be evil or righteous, and it's often hard to know which it is.

Moses becomes expert at limiting the outcome of God's outbursts. God repeatedly manifests rage as plagues. Emotional-spiritual plagues often took physical form in ancient times. Oedipus's patricide and incest brings a plague on Thebes, cured by the purification of truth, self-wounding, and exile. Pinchas's sword stops a plague, but so do Moses' supplications and arguments. Through his grief or cajoling reason or a combination of both, Moses often calms God and restricts the damage. It is as if God, at times, represents global emotionality, spreading boundlessly, with Moses a braking function.

God blusters and threatens total annihilation. In *Numbers* recalcitrant Hebrews arouse ire. In *Genesis* nearly all humanity is threatened, then this or that city or group of peoples or individuals. In *Numbers,* the people of the covenant, amplified through Mosaic law, were supposed to take over Canaan, where immorality was rampant. The Israelites were agents of God against the godless, in danger of sinking to the level of those they were supposed to teach, kill, or supplant. They were ever in danger of being wiped out themselves as God's rage rained on many objects. Israelites did not always need outside help in sinking to lower levels. Life's hardships — for example, desert homelessness — exacerbated faithlessness to the point where God's annihilation drive was piqued and renewal required mixtures of wonders and violence.

Rage spreads boundlessly, comes up against barriers, spends itself, diminishes spontaneously, seeks other paths, reverses directions, turns against self or other. A psychospiritually sensitive individual may wonder if, partly, God's rage reflects our self-hate associated with degraded being. Rage at self for a fallen existence easily translates into rage at others and vice versa. Rage at self tries to excise the moral cause of fallenness. Like Pinchas's sword, it aims at self-corruption. This attempt at cure underlies the notion that plagues Sophocles' Oedipus: corruption can be cured by exile, evil can be excised, on the order of cutting out an infected body part.

Thus Oedipus acts as lightning rod, container, scapegoat, a circumscribed locale through which moral corruption can be evacuated. That self-knowledge plays a role in this process does not change the underlying structure of the "cure." To purify the state of self or society by getting rid of corrupted parts (individuals, groups, inner tendencies, bad behavior) does not solve basic problems posed by our makeup. Evil is not so easily localized. Sophocles bequeaths to us raw materials for further work, which Freud picks up on. Appetite and repulsion regarding incest, infanticide, parenticide, fused with many forms of self-recrimination and defiance, are served up on platters by Sophocles and Freud for further digestion. Taking in such forces and discovering more about them seems a less lethal course than repetitious self-evacuation (exile).

God the father and bridegroom. Israel the children and bride. The Sabbath, too, may be a bride, as may God's presence, a certain fluidity of imagery. To all appearances, the marriage between God and Israel is a bad one, beset by chronic fighting, rages, injury, repair, starting over. It is as if the worst is maximized, also the best. Many are killed for infidelity but with some (the "remnant," or, in rabbinical Judaism, the pious, the very holy or righteous or tsadikkim) the bond is strengthened, raised, sanctified. The bond may grow in ordinary people too. Repentance is always open, the possibility of rediscovering the God connection is always there. And if all known channels close, unknown ones open.

Can repentance modify rage? For a time, more or less. Anger builds, rage happens, like the mounting of sexual tension or addictive craving. The cycle of rage and repentance can be costly. But occasionally repentance takes root and a change begins. Little by little, perhaps over a number of years, a shift of direction has consequences. Breakdowns, reversions occur, with quicker recovery time and greater flexibility. A repentant heart can't stay stuck in rageful positions too long or rigidly. There are too many marvels waiting to be tasted.

Korach might have cried from his bones and heart, "Moses, we are breaking; the Law is too harsh. It is grinding us down. We must have something softer, a change." Instead, Korach's precocious mind and sophistic arguments attempted to deconstruct law to absurdity. The heart-God connection is lacking. Korach is too much of a smartass. Bilam, too, tries to think or talk his way out of what heart knows. David and Jacob symbolize the heart-God connection, however serious their failings. Moses' whole life is devoured by God. This God intensity, loving God with all your heart, soul, might, mind—is missing in Korach, Bilam, Zimri. Bilam tries sophistry, but God breaks through it. Korach discovers smart arguments aren't the last (or first) word in what God is about.

Yet rabbinical law places limits on Pinchas's rage. The priestly class did not have a holy temple to practice in after their temple was twice destroyed. Prayer and good deeds replaced ritual sacrifice; local houses of study and worship took the place of a central temple. The descendents of the Hebrews no longer were one body marching toward the dream of Jerusalem and the Holy Temple, a dream worked out in fine detail but not foolproof. The human factor proved elusive. Instead of forming centrally organized political, military, judicial, and priestly groups, the people who became the Jews scattered like seeds over the face of the earth.

It is said the first temple was destroyed because of idolatry (infidelity to God, assimilation), the second because of causeless enmity between Jew and Jew. With the central priesthood lost and the voice of prophecy dimmed, how could one tell, if a Jew killed another in righteous rage, who was on God's side? Not all people can be Pinchas. Who has Moses' vision? Who can be his right arm? We need protection from one another, respect for differences. Rabbis tried to bind the murderous impulse with restrictions, since lines between a Pinchas and a fanatic began to fade. More room had to be given to the possibility of being wrong in committing and prosecuting acts of murder.

There is a story of a rabbi who, aroused to anger, reviewed the laws and commentaries related to justified and unjustified anger and its expression. Before he finished turning the arguments this way and that, his anger dissipated. Psychoanalysis is premised on the idea that culture binds passions and that language can rework the ways psychic energy is structured. The Torah tries to regulate affect by stories, history, prophesy, poetry, and laws. Love may be central, but God's rage is a showstopper. The Bible is replete with rage (God's, ours) and attempts to bind, direct, or modulate it. It does not solve the problem by laws or love or art but highlights the challenges that the enduring fact of rage presents. It puts a marker on rage, a kind of tracer, handing it to future generations for experience, meditation, and study.

The play of rage and grief also runs through Greek tragedy, which mourns what humans do to themselves and each other (and what God, Fate, Destiny do to all). The skein of destiny for Oedipus relies on road rage as one of its triggers (Oedipus killing his father on the road in macho dispute over the right-of-way). God's road rage in the Bible plays havoc when humans don't go the way

He wants. Rage tends to find limits in the play of interactive forces. One individual's rage limits another's. At times, rage transforms through dialogue, as when Moses talks God out of wrath or Moses' fury transforms through God's word. Moses and God dampen the effects of each other's rage. Each must deal with loss in the face of desire. God opens and limits access to Moses' heart's desire (e.g., seeing, not entering, the Promised Land). The Hebrew people arouse and frustrate God's hopes as a way of life. Personalities block total fulfillment of the desire and rage they arouse.

What does one do with the fierce God-force that permeates life? Looking the other way helps a little sometimes. But with all the little gods running around bumping into, or trying to gain advantage from, one another, with all the flare-ups of infinities of rage — the challenge is, indeed, passed on to us and we will pass it on to others. But right now, this moment, we work with it as best we can.

So much is fused in God's personality: rage, love, compassion, punishment, creativity, admonition, discussion, goodness, omniscience, omnipotence, suffering, light beyond anything we see, joy beyond imaginable ecstasy, the list goes on. Add to that our responses, and we have something approximating nearly all the emotions the soul can experience. There may be emotions the Bible leaves out, but it comes close to covering, one or another way, all the important ones.

It is easy to sentimentalize God, as movies have shown. And easy to subjectivize Him, as psychoanalysis does. The idea that we make God in our image, that He is our projection, is an old one. Mystics and meditators have long noted that we pour ourselves into God, fill Him with our concepts and imaginings, that even our best notions of God fall short and probably are idolatrous. It did not take Freud to point out that God is who we wish to be.

It is not enough to dismiss God by saying He is our anthropomorphic creation. Too much is missed by such a bypass. We have poured into God composites of emotions, modes of relating, states of being. God, partly, is a sedimentation, condensation, fossil store of psychical states spanning thousands of years. By dissecting God we add more to wonder about in our spiritual museum.

For one obsessed with God, it is surprising to discover that many do not care about God, lack the God-sensation—do not "feel" God —nor is God important to their thinking. God does not seem necessary for moral or satisfactory living. People get along well without Him. It may seem, then, that God is a matter of constructs, imaginings, styles of relating, sensibilities, emotional bearing. Nevertheless, there are people who do experience a sense of the living God, a wondrous, at times terrifying, uplifting sense of grace, the work of providence. For some God does and for some God doesn't play an important role in how life feels.

Sometimes I think one is better off without God, that God is the most evil notion ever invented. Belief in God—God on one's side, oneself on God's side—has been devastating, wreaking havoc between peoples. Holy wars, God help us! The idea of eternal damnation as a means to intimidate people or justify murder and domination—ghastly. The history of religious wars sickens the stomach, infuriates the soul, breaks the heart.

Racial and religious persecution (the two often fuse but are not identical) have more to them than lust for territory, protection of boundaries, and the rush of economic and political desire (though all of these are involved). On the one hand, many people feel a hatred of differences associated with dread of contagion, oneness, pollution. Germs of the other's otherness will infect and destroy what one imagines most real about one's group or individual existence.

On the other hand, there are some individuals who feel so on the brink of obliteration that from them there is nothing left to salvage. One of the most awful things in the world is for an individual to feel damned. Such blistering, radical despair exists today in spite of everything prophets said about it and in spite of contemporary medication. Prophets believe a change of heart is possible. By a shift of attitude, sins are washed away, one becomes as new. But there are people who feel such a possibility is closed to them because they are doomed forever.

One such individual came to my office after hospitalization, heavily dosed with medication. A sharp panic suffused him, yet he seemed dull and rigid. He numbed himself in the face of chronic intensity and felt polluted with wrong choices, no choices, weakness. God's voice told him what to do, and he could not follow it. He feared it would kill him. By not following it, he was lost forever. Either he must give himself to God and risk death or hold back and go to hell. In a voice at once panicky and dull, he tells me he is a lost soul, incurably sick morally and psychically, paralyzed by evil imaginings, outside forgiveness and grace, soul and mind sealed by a verdict that is final. I suggested he may have God and the devil mixed up, and he looked at me with a moment's interest.

While it is not legitimate to equate a man's psychosis with God's personality, there is much to learn zigzagging between what we imagine about ourselves and what we imagine about God. Drawing on some psychoanalytic concepts, it is possible to imagine this man's God as a fusion of id-superego elements preempting ego functions. An enormous aggressive onslaught is launched as judgment against self. Functions such as thinking and judgment are co-opted by runaway judgmentalism. It is as if superego swallowed ego and id, channeling them through tyrannical versions of itself. Instead of mutually supportive structures in generative symbiosis, all are parasitic on all as destructive plagues hit personality, deforming capacities.

Nevertheless, in the mixture of dread and certainty, doubt remains, signaling latent complexity. In the psychotic's obsessive spins, doubt is paralyzing and makes the individual feel contempt for weakness (his own and others). But the fact that personality ever doubts itself creates an opportunity for something more to happen. In a way, my psychotic patient is saved by his inability to act. It is part of his illness to temporize, put off, delay the moment of reckoning. But this very need to postpone leaves the door slightly open.

Years of despairing, devastating lament must be waded through. It is hideous to see how personality seizes on ideas of eternity and forecloses development. Such a totalitarian, unyielding God attacks mind and being, and one does not have the strength or ability to appease it. One cannot make the persecutory God happy. No matter what one imagines oneself doing, it will never be enough. This is not a God capable of looking at creation (especially the human self) as good and declaring a day of rest (Sabbath point of soul).

I get an image of radioactive seed implantation, a particular form of cancer therapy. Instead of therapy, I picture radioactive seeds as cancerous particles spreading through personality, seeds of panic-rage altering space-time via high-velocity particle collision, fusion of panic-rage in every psychic pore. Morality becomes a hideous caricature, finding in every moment reasons to condemn self. Too often such atrocious states of being penetrate the social body, usurp political structures, and play a role in the destructive fusion of military and economic life. They are not confined to hospitals or doctors' offices or agonized groupings of solitary individuals. Under the guise of national, racial, economic, military concerns, psychotic dynamics are normalized, as the pace of daily life could not continue without them.

Nevertheless, it often is part of psychosis to rev up the sense of goodness at the same time that self suffers obliteration. Disintegration into goodness characterizes certain mystical experiences. However, in psychosis the individual seems stuck, rigidly disintegrating and rigidly trapped by hypergood. Rather than enriching personality growth, goodness and the self glue to each other and are stillborn. Vision of the Good works overtime counteracting malignant annihilation. Magnified ideal feeling at the self's core attempts to placate, drown, or mute magnified deformity.

This stillborn quality plays a role in the innocence-corruption polarity so prevalent in psychotic character. Many psychotic individuals seem "innocent" and condemn life for impurities. They are tuned in to beatific soul-feeling that reality cannot match. Inability or refusal to give themselves to dirty living lends them an "unborn" quality. At the same time, they feel eternally corrupted. They fail to live up to the best in them and are convinced that they have succumbed to a pact with the devil taking them downward.

In psychosis certain slivers of self stand out like raw bones of personality. Addiction to a double sense of innocence-corruption plays itself out many ways. Corrupted aspects of self conduct smear campaigns, attacking the innocent self as hypocritical, vain, incapable. Innocence is paralyzed, ashamed of goodness, thrown into doubt because evidence indicates that good fails to actualize in real life. The cynical self rips apart good acts, knowing aggression is part of any activity. Corrupted self elements form part of the psychic substratum. In psychosis both the good and corrupt are totalized, each is everything, so that movement is impossible, or, perhaps more accurately, intensity and burnout coincide, so that one moves like crazy staying in the same place. One feels too corrupt to be allowed to live, too innocent to get into life.

The stainless-stained theme has a history going as far back as religious memory and occupies many pages in the Bible. Many laws regarding ritual and practice tell how to cleanse individuals and groups of impurities. Some are prescriptive, some postscriptive. There are laws for purifying diseased walls and utensils as well as people. Laws of cleanliness and sacrifice. Pollution spans physical, moral, behavioral, and psychical levels with rules to remedy nearly any situation. Sometimes death wipes out stains; sometimes the cure is less drastic.

The mystery of the red heifer is exemplary in certain ways. After Korach (see "Pinchas Afterwaves" above) is defeated and priestly lines defined, lists of laws are given, culminating in the red heifer statutes. God tells Moses and Aharon that the children of Israel should bring a faultless, unblemished young cow to Eliezar the priest, Aharon's son. Details are given for sacrificing the virgin heifer (which even two brown hairs disqualify), with the odd property that whoever participates in the rites becomes impure. The rites of purity defile in this case. Provisions are given for cleansing defilement arising from conducting parts of the purification ritual.

It is a little like the story of one person after another sticking to the person he is trying to free, as the number of people stuck to one another mounts. Each person tries to purify another defiled by the red heifer purification ritual, only to require purification in turn. The ultimate object is to make a mixture of the red heifer's ashes and spring water to be sprinkled on those defiled by contacting or sharing space with a dead body. A sort of purification-defilement hot potato. Being with a corpse defiles, but so do the cleansing rituals. It is as if there is uncleanness that gets passed from one to another, a stain that can never be removed. A community of effort is needed to diffuse it. We need each other to help cleanse the sins with which we infect one another. We defile each other by helping one another, but helping is our path to mutual cleansing too.

Traditional commentators conclude the statutes revolving around the red heifer remain a mystery. It may be that these rituals make up for the sin of the golden calf. But in the end they have weight because God spoke them. Their very impenetrability highlights a mysterious bond with God.

Nevertheless, there is much to draw out from the red heifer "paradox." Our sense of purity gets externalized in objects, here a sacrificial object. In this instance purity is pure red. An animal ordinarily used for meat and milk (which, according to rabbinical strictures, must not be eaten together), work and procreation, is here reserved for purifying individuals stained by death. Death purifies, death stains. Fire and water purify. The ashes of the pure heifer unite with fresh water, doubly, triply pure. Red? Often a symbol of passion or hot emotion, red with eros, red with rage. And, of course, the red heifer must have been strikingly beautiful, a sensuous treat. In attempting to purify death, a symbol of passion (part of one's tie to life) is nullified. Is this part of deep symbol logic—cleanse contact with death by erasing the blaze of life?

Everything is once removed, as if keeping one's own death at a distance. It is, after all, an animal that is sacrificed, not oneself, a substitution. Animal for self, and animal self, passional being transmuted in service of higher power ("yoked" to the Torah).

Burning the red heifer, also, is a kind of sacrifice of purity. As suggested above, in psychosis one is paralyzed by a double sense of purity-corruption, feeling too pure to live, too corrupt to have the right to live. Burning the heifer signifies a willingness to live a real life, the pure animal being a kind of dream animal, an ideal state, raised for ritual rather than ordinary living. Psychotic demand for purity makes real living impossible. Sacrifice of the red heifer suggests a wish to be less tyrannized by madness.

However, things are not so easy. If only one got rid of death, evil and madness by sacrificing a dream animal. If only that were what it took to rid oneself of stain or burn out purity. The red heifer condenses wishes to be rid of purity and corruption, a double tyranny that scars the self. A purifying ritual may work for a while, but defilement mounts again. Fire and water offer no permanent antidote for what ails the soul, although it may work against disease for a time (e.g., play a role in sanitation). The red heifer dilemma brings the interweaving between defilement-purity into focus, as obsessive demands for purity try to keep up with possibilities of defilement. What cleanses one person defiles another. In psychic reality it is also likely that purity and defilement are one, coincide, linear readings of ineffable fusion.

The obsessiveness in religious ritual described by Freud blossoms in the red heifer statutes. The feeling of purity getting spoiled seems characteristic of experience in certain keys. A semi-free-floating sense of purity gets attached to many areas and is ever subject to damage. Death contaminates, but so may sex under certain conditions, or anger, or violence (which may purify and/or defile). That contact with a corpse can lead to infection does not explain extravagant magnification of sanitation precautions into indissoluble longing for purity of soul.

"O my God, the soul you have given me is pure," the heart bursts in prayer. Pure point of soul—God-connection, incessant infusion of purity. What would we feel like without a sense of purity? Is it ever totally gone? And its twin, corruptibility—would we be better off without it?

From a literalist perspective, one might say the sense of purity-corruptibility arose in relation to danger (e.g., health vs. illness) and signaled survival directions. But what sort of being transfers health prescriptions for the body to a sense of infinite soul? Is soul a derivative formation of ineffable consciousness, growing out of a sensation of pure awareness? Why would this be ethically tinged?

Again the literalist might argue that ethics is a practical matter, a way of regulating social relations, limiting murder, greed, possessiveness. To do to others what you'd like them to do to you is a form of damage control. Cooperation and altruism have survival value. This takes the mystery out of ethics and frees one from bondage to the numinous.

"Not so quick," cries the soul. "No one denies the importance of practicality. That's not what I'm talking about. Yes, there is practical ethics, survival ethics. We can't get along without it, not now, not yet, perhaps not ever. But I bring a surplus of—well, something else. I am myself throbbing radiance. To denude ethics of mystery is naive. The dagger of ethics thrusts deep, its point moving ever deeper as we trace it. We can find neither beginning nor end, but have lots of ideas about it and a basic feeling that's hard to describe.

"The kingdom of heaven in you, soul's garden, pleasure in the goal region, joy, ecstasy, overflowing cup, abundance, effulgence, plenitude, blissful emptiness, just so nothingness. More. More.

" 'An ethics of the face,' says Levinas. The face of the other, opening to infinity, infinite openness. Experiencing the preciousness of existence a face upholds. The face of the other opens the self. Yes, practice emerges. To guard the rights of the other protects the self's access to the infinite and grows out of that access. A kind of divine selfishness, selfishness of inclusion, the divinity of the other self one's guarantor."

In obsessive ethics purity goes haywire. Self gets dirty faster than we can clean it. A hysterical underpinning clings to obsessive ethics. One gets hysterically upset over the untoward consequences of a botched cleansing, since death, disease, or bad fortune may result. Emotional storms cling to obsessive rituals. Effort multiplies, obsessive hysteria and hysterical obsessiveness goad each other, depression resulting. Moments of success border on mania. Failure triggers rage or grief or fear. Repeated lapses and mess-ups can lead to the worst ending of all, a sense of despair about oneself— one will never be good enough for God. To somewhat magnify and distort the heifer message: one is doomed by efforts to clean oneself and others.

This sounds like Saint Paul's picture of self-defeating law addiction, although Jesus said he came to fulfill the law. Fulfillment as, partly, liberation through faith. To a certain extent, soul is self-cleansing. We do not know how this works but are told that charity, repentance, and prayer play a role. Such actions reach out to God directly, from body, heart, mind. The fusion of obsessive, hysterical, paranoid, depressive ethics fades. A soul clearing opens. The mystic aspect of soul sees God, feels God, hears God, touches God.

For me, this is the essence of Jesus' message. There is heaven in you. Open your eyes, open your ears. What is the great mantra of Israel? "Listen and hear the One." Love God with all your heart, mind, soul, might. Love the One with All. This is the contact that cleanses soul, the source of soul's self-cleansing capacity.

Here mystical Judaism and mystical Platonism come together. We are at the doorstep (heartstep, mindstep) of Plato's Vision of the Good, homebase of the soul. Goodness pours into the universe, fills soul, ever cleansing, directly from God. At this moment, in this place, only the Good is real. Affirmation is part of the good sense (sense of basic goodness), effortless, not extraneous. Freedom is translated through grace.

Where does the bad stuff go while this is happening? The fearful self and its obsessive, hysterical, paranoid, depressive ethics, periodically blossoming into an ethics of rage? It doesn't vanish forever. It resurfaces, reappears, grips one again. Perhaps it is always gripping one in the background, even when its hold diminishes. Even when one is sucking on God's peace.

**W**hy does stubbing one's toe set one off in the direction of rage? Most of the time one does not become absolutely rageful in the face of minor self-injury, but there is an immediate rise of anger past irritability, toward fury, in response to frustration. On an immediate reflex level, one draws back in the face of pain. But there is more.

One is furiously upset with oneself. One may blame the chair one ran into and throw it down. But one also feels something like, "How could I be so stupid or careless or unobservant or... How could *I* do *that?!*" As if *I* ought to be above or beyond such mishaps.

There is self-to-self drama, internal monologue betraying deep expectation. One tells oneself, "You shouldn't have done that." The *I* blaming *You*—subject blaming itself as object, perhaps as naughty, incompetent, or clumsy child.

The tendency to self-blame can become impacted. An inadequate child is installed within and acts as a magnet for mishap and mayhem. It is a matter of structural indifference whether causality (blame) is attributed to I or you inside or outside. Pronouns, subjects and objects, may be variously distributed but the basic structure—the disposition to blame—remains steadfast.

You spills into I, as well as I into you. In the face of permeability, the I may try to separate blame from itself into a you packet (whether a you as part of self or other). Insofar as permeability cannot be stopped, blame may boomerang or spread. As you and I leak into each other, the I is spoiled by blame it tries to get rid of. Insofar as the process spirals, blame becomes tinged with self-hate. The I poisons itself by its own tendencies, by tendencies in the psychic field it grows in. Correlatively, a demeaned or persecuted object (inside or outside self) becomes a habit (someone or something to blame).

As the I and object defile each other, one loses sight of a hidden should: "This should not be happening to me. I ought not be doing this to myself. I ought to be exempt from processes I emerge from or plunge into." A spontaneous tendency toward megalomania attaches to a sense of purity and control and issues in a barely sensed judgment: I ought to be above myself, not subject to processes that make me up and that I am partly aware of.

Some of the difficulty and challenge is that awareness separates out of the emotional matrix and becomes aware of itself as pure awareness, awareness as such. This self-focusing can be a source of joy. But too often awareness is trapped by, and overidentifies with, its capacity to observe and judge and ends up tormenting personality. It can reach an extreme: I am or ought to be above everything. Rage signifies cracks in the system. Pure I-am-I or I-less awareness stubs its toe on everything.

Body rage magnifies into transcendental rage. I-God fusion (basic forms: I am I; I am God; I am not-I) acts as unconscious transformer, revving emotional tendencies toward infinities. To stub one's toe on the universe triggers rage.

There is holy wrath in the infant's scream.

Rage against injustice. Rage against painful facts.

It is a rage that may attach to political causes, rising against perceived unfairness or fueling the tyrant's position. Either side of a have/have not barrier has a foot in rage.

The fearful, rageful scream of the infant is rooted in outrage and insufficiency—often outrage *at* insufficiency. Relative helplessness and megalomania go together. One may not cause the other, but they play off each other. Megalomania is furious at helplessness, and helplessness can arouse megalomania. Megalomania tries to drown the helplessness it feeds off of. The baby's scream combining both is never far from the surface for all our lives.

There was a time in my life when I gained a lot by screaming. I was in a bioenergetic therapy class in which I screamed and screamed and screamed. At one point, the leader complained to my therapist. As used as she was to screaming, I frightened her. It was just after President Kennedy's murder. Sometimes I screamed, "Kill, Kill, Kill." This was too much for the class leader. It was over the line.

But those classes were terribly important to me. They really did what they claimed to do, get me in touch with my body, open body self in new ways. One afternoon, another leader made an intervention that changed my life. He put me over his back, back to back, and my chest opened. Feelings streamed through sensation fields. My heart opened. I felt my heart was a vagina opening. He asked to say what I experienced, and when I told him about my heart as vagina he got defensive, withdrew, and shut me up. Whatever I was experiencing was not what he had in mind. I have the fantasy that later he told me he was paranoid. It was well known (though not to me then) that he had a paranoid streak. Nevertheless, he was excellent.

My therapist reassured the female leader that I was no threat, but something changed, and, in spite of my regrets, I saw the handwriting on the wall. The male leader left for California and, although I hung in there, unwilling to give up what had been so good, the class gradually waned in significance for me.

Now, nearly forty years later, threads aroused or highlighted then have undergone much evolution, growing in significance, essential elements in a larger tapestry of self. Raging scream and vaginal heart, strange twins in the shock and thrill of self.

I also tried some primal scream therapy, where I could scream to my heart and soul's content. The practitioner did not freak out, but I found his interpretations somewhat limiting. A certain contraction in my being remained intact. Nevertheless, raging has helped fill me out—tissues, muscles, glands, nerves, fibers of my being. One feels a certain strength in raging. But this kind of work left me raw, exposed, and, paradoxically, a lesser version of myself, in spite of all the experience of might. I'm glad I did it and glad I went beyond it, although some form of body work stayed with me all my life.

I found in Winnicott a very different approach to the scream within. He recognized the importance of the scream becoming part of dream work. A patient with skin eruptions and strained body states became aware of her need to scream. She contacted a failed, stillborn, or vanishing scream, a scream she was "always not experiencing." As Winnicott suggested, the scream that might make her well was "the great non-event of every session." In contrast to my more extroverted screaming, his patient, at last, dreamt of screaming and felt the better for it.

Winnicott felt the scream she was looking for was "the last scream just before hope was abandoned." What is important here is not simply screaming, but *inability, not* being able to scream, various nuances of losing screaming. The capacity to scream cannot be taken for granted. Winnicott depicts a situation in which a mother does not respond to a baby's cry, until the point comes when the baby feels it is no use and screaming fails in its purpose. Communication at the level of screaming is jeopardized. Therapy provides a situation in which growth can occur toward the point where screaming can be felt, hope retrieved, although the scream, by this time, may be inaudible, purely emotional. It is, after all, the emotional scream that matters most, feelings touched by feelings.

In therapy, the lost scream surfaces because it has a partner, someone who hears it. A therapist knows about soul screams. Winnicott speaks of the scream linking psyche and soma. A positive function of "crying, screaming, yelling, angry protest" can be "immense strengthening of the psycho-somatic interrelationship" and less need of artificially keeping oneself in life. Winnicott believes his patient's ability to dream of the scream she lost "only becomes possible as a result of the analysis, in which hope about screaming returns," enabling contact with healthier elements of her life.

For Winnicott, dreaming plays an important role in psychic aliveness, and therapy plays an important role in supporting dreaming. I wonder now whether deep dreaming activity was a missing link in my too easy ability to scream. It is not altogether fair to compare two such different cases, yet I feel, as much as I got out of screaming, it rode over certain insufficiencies, masked broken links with myself. The intensity and duration in which Winnicott's patient had to bear the sense of a lost, absent or missing scream paved the way for deeper appreciation for the *feeling* of screaming when it began to appear. I believe now that actually screaming can interfere with the unfolding of the felt scream, although it may not need to. The dream scream opens the possibility of *feeling* connecting waking and sleeping.

After connecting with her dream scream, Winnicott's patient was able to sing in public and protest her therapist's failings. The surge in body aliveness I felt in screaming has stood me in good stead throughout my life. In time, I dropped deeper into body and self, sensing unending nuances of what it feels like to be alive, the might of rage part of the flow of feeling. Whether the movement is outside-in or inside-out, therapy offers the possibility of letting the sense of outrage and anguish turn into communicative links with oneself and others.

*Bion's Big Bang*

Bion writes of "an intense catastrophic emotional explosion O" in which aspects of personality are "instantaneously expelled to vast distances from their point of origin and from each other." There are various ways to understand Bion's writings on "explosion O."

The beginning of our psychic universe may be likened to a big bang, an explosion into consciousness or psychic life, with a certain violence part of birth and the growth processes. But the explosion depicted in the passage at hand is part of destructive processes, a damaging or maiming of psychic capacities. In a manner analogous to Winnicott, although very much in his own fashion, Bion depicts the dying of a scream.

A nourishing situation turns destructive, and a scream replaces well-being. Screaming functions, for a time, as a link between personalities. First breast or food (something sweet and good, goodness itself), then scream—one link substituting for another. As destruction spirals, the scream dies out. There may be refusal to scream, negativism, an angry no-scream. But the explosive process explodes the hating will and dissolves into stupor and oblivion, no scream, no personality, zero. Maximum-minimum emotion are one, as both signal a ghastly, traumatic process.

Here is a situation in which screaming does no good. No one hears it. The self of the scream is not responded to. Rage may continue for a while, feeding on itself, finally obliterating itself. The result may be a personality we call burnt out, wounded, hardened, mean, or weak. Mean and weak spots abound in all of us. Burnt-out rage, rage that never ends. An explosion that goes on and on creating havoc, yet is emotionally ineffectual. One becomes embalmed in an explosion lost in space.

What is worse, the ability to digest what is happening is injured. It is as if the traumatizing process also damages the ability to digest trauma. Our psychic digestive system is, at once, wounded and in shock. This is a situation, perhaps, more devastating than the one Winnicott depicts. If dreaming helps to focus and process emotional impacts and dreamwork, as part of our emotional digestive system, is damaged, the dream that needs to be dreamt (including the scream that needs to be dreamt) is undone by the explosive force it needs to contain. Our ability to process emotions may be warped or damaged by the emotional force it is asked to process.

Unending rage, for example, can destroy the apparatus that needs to work with it.

Often damage and rage in one part of a system escapes notice and shows up somewhere else. For instance, an unconsciously damaged, enraged being or group determined to win may indeed taste the joy of triumph, while outrage festers at a distance, building counterexplosive force. If explosiveness is the link between people, the very binder ensures further destructiveness.

In such a situation, the challenge to therapy is immense. The therapist, I believe, carries an important personal and social function as spokesperson for the value of dreaming emotional life, a step toward being better able to experience and process emotional impacts. We inflict on others impacts we cannot process ourselves. As a group the human race must work toward being able to shoulder these impacts and learn what to do with the explosive force we are. The pages of this book nibble at these impacts, feed our psychic digestive system, stimulate emotional digestion.

Janice flings herself on the couch in a rage, bangs the cushions with her fists, smashes the wall, hurts herself, makes her knuckles bleed. She goes limp. She weeps, grows calm. After a long silence she says, almost chanting, "You can live as long as you don't take any space. You can dive so long as you don't use any air."

She chants more sayings, but I don't remember them. She talks about her love for deep diving, worlds undersea. She says sadly, "I use less air than my dive masters."

The voice tells her in many forms, she can live as long as she uses nothing from life, the barest minimum possible. What does such a voice have in common with the voice Moses heard, that stamps our beings?

"I'm more at home underwater than on land," she says.

"I'm more at home in the unconscious," I think.

---

"Rage runs through it," I say.

Joe totally agrees, as if it is a bit of relief to hear it, see it, know it, feel it. It is right before him.

He speaks of one of his kids not doing homework, messing up the house. Joe's wife reacts angrily, rage spirals. Joe feels she fuels the boy's fury by her stiff way of making him do what she wants, her inability to cut him any slack. Everything he likes is a threat — video games, TV, time wasters, mind degraders. She can't stop punishing him.

Joe himself likes video games and wastes time. He seems to get more pleasure being with the kids without having to have a task to complete. He values undemanding moments. Now the ante is upped. There are complaints the boy in question is having rage bursts in school, when teachers make demands. No one is sure what to do. Maybe therapy for the boy? For the family? For our society?

Joe complains about his wife. He reacts to her much as his son does, or vice versa. They often enrage each other. He is not home enough, and when he is home, she feels he does the wrong things. He feels she is more controlling than responsive and takes no responsibility for her erratic feelings and lapses (she spends too much money, makes too little, neglects tasks, scolds the kids for neglecting tasks, must always be right). It doesn't take much for them to trigger each other. Rage spreads through the house like fire in dry wood. Yet the house is not without love.

---

Barney complains of "an obsessive voice that keeps hacking at me when I'm with women, telling me what to do, not to do, commenting on my faults, scoring me for what I'm doing wrong. Like subvocals in a Woody Allen movie, only worse because there's no letup. I can't have a moment when I can just be with a woman and let things happen."

"And when you're alone?"

"It's relentless. It makes me scared of taking trips. 'You're going to die. Your plane will crash.' Anything I want to plan—there's threat of death. But there are better times when I'm alone, too. Times I draw, listen to music, feel a sense of creativeness. You never know how long it'll last, how fragile. A wrong move and the threats come back. You never know what the wrong move will be."

Barney spent years in therapy. He discovered or attributed depths and breadths of meaning to his problems, went over childhood roots endlessly. He tried behavior therapy, which helped, to a point. Behavior modification taught him to see the relentless voice as part of a background of toxic sludge or noise—don't get stuck in it, don't pay it too much attention. It will pass, and even if it persists, he can keep functioning.

Yet the drive to understand would not go away, even with evidence that understanding does not make the problem go away. The wish to understand persisted like a bad habit. I wondered if understanding and the voice joined together, a wedding of sorts. Voice attacks, mind tries to understand. A kind of psychic cement, mixed with rage-fear.

I was imagining the marriage of understanding-attack when Barney began going over (again) his guilt for "eclipsing my father, having my mother to myself, asking my mother to divorce my father. There was a time my father and I were close. We were close and then he was gone. Something happened between my mother and father. His affairs? Something put them at odds with each other, and I was brought into the conflict on my mother's side. She'd point to his rages, obvious proof he was the wrong one. But he and I remained close. After he left, I replaced him. My siblings knew I became the man. I was the one whose brains would take us out of Egypt, lead us to the promised land. My mother's hope. I didn't know there was such a hole in my life when my father left. In my own inflated soul I filled the space he left in me. But deep down I was devastated, a disaster. It took to the end of my twenties to manifest. Then I knew I was riddled. My father's rage shot through me like a canon, but his leaving tore me more. I was left with no protection, not even his rage. I was left with messianic imaginings that carried me only so far."

"Where does rage come from?" I asked.

"It's a reaction to a relation that's broken down. A disconnect. A reaction to disappearance, fear. A disconnect that is overwhelming, intolerable. An intolerable rupture, something broken that can't ever be repaired."

I think of the disconnect running through Barney's life, rage growing in holes, the voice that torments him, a rage funnel, clotted rage, a rage machine. And beneath, a heart longing for repair.

---

Analysis: Barney's mindvoice—disconnected rage, mentalized rage. Where is the rage in his body, his father's rage? His mother's rage was in her words and gestures, attitude, position. His father's body rage took up space Barney needed, space Barney's body rage needed. Barney's rage traveled upward. He was smarter than his father. He was going to beat life with his mind, while his father was condemned to a life of hard physical labor. Who won? Lost? Barney's rageful mindvoice attacks body warmth, passion, need, soul's creative loves.

"Where does rage come from?" A question to ask over and over.

––––––––

Milton says, "Rage feels safe. Like heroin—an instantaneous effect. It dulls pain, hypnotizes it away. All I have to do is be willing to live in that deadness like so many people. It makes me want to throw up."

––––––––

Linda's raging at me subsides. She's been furious but does not know why. Maybe it's because I'm not her lover. Perhaps she is warding off the realization that if I were her lover, she would still be a disturbance to herself. At the moment I am the one causing her pain. But she would be in pain whether or not I were in her life. Being so filled with rage is painful. Then there is a bit of opening. "It's hard to love because of when it stops," she says. She speaks of moments when love comes but her lover isn't loving or his interest is elsewhere. She means more. She talks about loving and falling off the end of the earth, because in love one falls off the end of love. She becomes very quiet, draws back, sinks into herself, regroups, brightens. "Better get used to it or be alone," she whispers.

She did not blow up for nearly a month after that moment.

––––––––

Milton says, "The biggest difference is I feel anxiety more. I don't have to turn to rage as quickly. I feel more anxious, not less. I show love for my wife more, and she feels loved. I grew up with people who didn't sound like they loved each other, even if sometimes they did. The word "love" was mostly hollow, insane. There was nothing in it. Love meant madness, emptiness. You'd reach for it, and it was crazy or wasn't there.

"I take my dog out and feel his excitement when he sees another dog. That's what I miss. His excitement makes me angry, triggers an impulse to murder, kill the excitement that dies in me, that is stillborn. I think how dead my mother was and want to murder her—the pain of hollow, crazy love, vacuousness, worse than no love at all. She was never there inside when I went to touch her with my insides. Yet I have what I dread. I have fierce attachments, my children, my wife, my work, maybe you, others in my mind—ferocity of attachment. As dead as I am, painful as it is, I'm fiercely attached to *experiencing*. The worst thing is *experience ceases,* and I want to be dead because *nothing happens*. I'm not ongoing. Everything stops.

"This is where I feared I'd be. I dreaded ending up in this spot —unable and not knowing how to live with such barrenness. Hate is ever filled with energy. I can stuff the barrenness with rage. For years rage brought relief. Now it increases the pain. I watch it stuff the loss. My rage signifies loss. Rage is endless because loss is endless.

"There must be rage that signifies might, conquest, power, being an emperor, a warrior. Strong rage, healthy rage. But now I feel even that rage stifles loss, postpones it, tries to make it vanish. My rage grew out of death, a poisonous death, suffocation, lack of enlivening feeling. I'm listening, looking for a hint of feeling I can believe, a hint of something good or true that rage doesn't suck up or vaporize. If rage is the only truth, then nothing is true. I can't believe in this rage, but I believe in nothing else.

"I don't stop. The feeling rage sucks on says there's more. But *more* tortures me too. I don't believe it's real. But I do . . . and it torments me."

———————

Milton: "There's been less pain in my bones, the visceral pain. More room. I'm more OK myself but am afraid of my impact on others, my poison. My snake."

Barney dreams he is dying. "My father is there, friendly, talking me into life. I was dying and he was friendly. What could *he* do?" Barney seems to depreciate his father's efforts. Too little, too late. He depreciates his dream.

He depreciates therapy, *his* life, his death-in-life. Life did not live up to his mother's inflated dream, or his own. Yet here is his dream father, not giving up on him.

Analysis: Rage is in the depreciation.

The dream is a fanning into life, part of therapy's goodwill, room for hell.

Barney dreams I'm cleaning his floors. Afterward, he cleans his floors too. He depreciates therapy and me and himself, but we keep working. I'm on my knees cleaning—which is OK with me. A floor of the psyche gets attention. Anna O called therapy "chimney sweeping," but we're moving toward ground level. Rage cleans, if put to good use. My example helps. I'm not afraid to get on my knees. He follows suit. We begin to undo contempt (his mother's, his own, his father's self-contempt), for his father as laborer, a chance to ground braininess.

Milton: "We made love. I felt the difference, really lovemaking, for the first time, almost the first. I never let myself get that open, where the feeling overtakes me, passes through my heart.

"Friends came over. I couldn't believe I was having a good time, a really good time. I'm afraid to say it, I had moments of living good without losing integrity, something I didn't think possible."

I knew when Milton said good, he meant good. A clearing in the rage.

Milton: "I had a client today who was so contracted, honest. I've been such a phony, trying to make everything feel OK, to keep connected with father, God. But when I contract, I don't feel as honest as I felt she was. My expansiveness is phony. But my contraction isn't true either.

"I believe in openness in principle, but we are so gnarled.

"I feel rage in my eyes, my neck. Rage keeps me separate. A tightening, self-tightening. It creates a felt boundary in my sensations and feelings. Rage keeps me separate, fights invasion. Contracting, tensing, tightening, fighting. It stops any mingling of wires, a fear of mingling of wires.

"I'm afraid my poison will be too much. You won't be able to metabolize it. As long as I can stay here, I can feel disorganized, disintegrated. It's happening here—I'm disintegrating. It's horrible but somehow manageable. It's in my stomach. If I lose the boundary, if I disintegrate, if I get absorbed [by you, by/with another person], I'd just have to throw my head back, roll my eyes, and I won't know anything anymore."

------

Milton: "Disintegrating protects me from getting absorbed.

"I'd have given anything for a special bond with my father instead of a black substrate, a black stomach pain that creates a boundary, even though it sucks everything into it.

"I imagine a special bond would have saved me, make me better. But my imagining is rage."

Rage grows out of a failure of the bond.

Rage prevents a better bond from forming.

Rage bonds or is part of a bonding process, one of the threads that knit together.

Rage rips at the knot it helps create.

------

Claudia lives in a field of rage. She dreams she asks the principal of her school to fix her, make her better. The woman says she won't.

Claudia is downcast and furious. The woman acted too good, superior, reticent, withholding. She refused to fix Claudia's feeling self, make her better. This implies she could, if she were so inclined. This is a lie in the dream, a misleading implication. The truth is she couldn't fix Claudia no matter how much she wanted to or how she tried. The dream is built on a delusion. Claudia is hurt—rage justified—by someone the dream puts in a position where she can't come through. The woman in power won't do something she really can't. She pretends she could if she would, but she hides in her own restriction.

The dream is steeped not only in disappointment and loss but also in delusional outrage. It posits a possibility that power cannot deliver but pretension glosses over.

Later in the session Claudia mentions that her mother always called her a "cold fish." The story is that Claudia pushed her mother away since infancy. When Claudia listens to herself, she hears, "Go away. Go away."

"I can't help feeling you're trying to make someone go away who couldn't be there anyway," I say (mother as cold fish).

Rage pushes away someone who shouldn't be there, reacts against invasiveness and toxic feeling, a response to real threat. But rage is also tinged with delusional mastery, imagining it is pushing away another one couldn't have, whose defects made healthy giving impossible (i.e., all or any of us, more or less).

Claudia opened a little more, face flushed—pleasure, actually joy, seeping into space that rage occupied.

---

Megalomania-vulnerability: twin veins of rage.

---

The poet rages against the coming of the night. He does not expect to stop death. No brakes here. If anything, the poem is an accelerator. It accelerates so that life pops out of death for an instant. Life stands alone, on its own merit. There is a point where rage acts as an accelerant. Then life takes over.

AFTERWORD

**W**e do not know what transformations rage will—or *can*—undergo. Frankly, we do not know what will happen when we monkey with emotions, but monkey around we must. To explore, push boundaries, com- bine, recombine, test, transfigure—nothing stops us. With our last wriggle, we try to experience more, taste life anew, a bit differently. We push against ourselves, through walls of self.

We experiment with explosive forces outside ourselves and learn something about turning switches on and off. But with so- cial, psychological, and, yes, mystical explosive forces, we're pretty much on our own. We have religion, myth, literature, art, neurol- ogy, chemistry, the social sciences to help us. We are driven to leave no stone unturned. Still, nothing substitutes for the way life feels and how we respond to this feeling.

After forty years of therapeutic work, I am convinced that neuroscience will not solve the problem of rage or emotional life in general. It may learn to turn rage on or off, even modulate it so it can be blended with other emotional currents. It may save a lot of lives, make many lives better. But in the end, the problem of emotions, rage in particular, will be in our hands, our lives. Whatever we learn about the switches, how we evaluate and use them has an ineradicable subjective element. Whether on or off medication, our lust to live from our own subjective center, our drive to taste our own reality, eggs us on. No one, finally, can *feel* our lives but us.

I may be hopelessly "retro," but the older I get, the more I value Freud's concern with hallucination. Some kind of hallucinatory/ delusional halo limes human experiencing. We have done our best to break through it or set it aside. At times we go too far, attempt-

( 164 )

ing to denude experience of subjectivity. We try to imagine what reality would be like if emotion did not color it, even suffer the delusion that emotions do not count as part of truth. Of course, to set subjectivity aside in the search for truth is a goal that can work against itself, since it is through consciousness that we have access to anything. Bearing in mind that our attempts are feeble and we really don't know what we're playing with, we have little choice but to familiarize ourselves, as best we can, with the experiential capacity that soaks our existence.

Freud imagines the baby hallucinates breast and good feed when it is hungry. There exists an image of satisfaction, a memory transformed into perception, and something more. Not only is a good, satisfying feed conjured up: the good state is maximized, infinitized—it is perfect, ideal, beatific. It is Freud's twist on the Socratic Vision of the Good, the ideal Goodness that drives the universe.

In one way or another, a sense of the ideal runs through Freud's account of transference—idealization of parent, self, lover, teacher, state, God. Or "perverse" idealization, say, of feces. In a way, the devil is an idealization of evil, pure evil. Pure instances of the evil in-clination are hard to find, but some events seem to come close. It is no accident that political and racial power appeal to pure or ideal standards to justify their cause. Freud opens the possibility of trac-ing hallucinatory threads in ideal feelings. The sense of the ideal may fuel love, uplift life, nourish faith, inspire beauty—but it also plays a role in fanning the most ghastly things humans do to one another.

Freud's story about the baby hallucinating the breast may be a fiction, but it points to a truth that needs to be assimilated. We may try to imagine bliss where there is agony, substituting one state for another. Rage intensifies when the beatific feed that is imagined turns out to be illusory. Hallucination binds and fuels rage, the latter increasing as the former breaks down. This is an extreme formulation of a thread that runs through life in muted forms.

We try to make ourselves feel better in the face of onslaughts of distress. In professional and social life, we put on our best face, act better than we are, hide fragmentation, doubt. We act in terms of images, selected intentions and stratagems, hoping to appear more whole than any person is. We foist off on others and ourselves hallucinatory versions of who we wish to be and get mad or laugh when these are pierced. We want to pass ourselves off as perfect feeds for each other, especially when what we dish out is indigestible.

Freud's vision runs through the body, binding glands with ideals. Something like ideal feeling is part of sensory streaming. The pleasure that teases the underside of skin, tantalizes pores of our body, strokes mucous membranes and movement of muscles, the eros that runs through our feeling life—fuses with the thrill of thinking, godly ecstasy, the swoon induced by beauty. This is not to reduce one to the other, to find the lowest common denominator. All realms inform each other. We are the kind of beings for whom thinking is exciting (if agonizing), for whom feeling opens worlds. Body and mind bind and free each other, spirit leaps through them.

Bion feels hallucination is a constant part of psychic activity. Whether or not this turns out to be correct in a literal way (and it may be!), such a strong formulation makes us think about what role hallucination might be playing in the dream of our lives. One function, emphasized by Bion, especially linked with "psychotic" pockets of personality, is a tendency to expel, get rid of, evacuate disturbance. In extreme form, since much experience is disturbing, the ghastly culmination of hallucinatory functioning is to rid ourselves of the trouble (and delight) of experiencing as such, in effect, evacuating the capacity to live our lives.

In a less extreme form, the tendency to expel is adaptive. It plays a role in regulating stimulation. Without some such ability, we would be incessantly overwhelmed by floods of internal and external events. In this sense, hallucination is part of our psychic filtration system. However, Bion is interested in what happens when the tendency to expel mushrooms.

One scenario involves sensitivity too raw to bear emotional impacts and/or emotional impacts too devastating for sensitivity. To some degree, sensitivity is sacrificed for survival. There are ways survival requires increased insensitivity. Much of the time we are variable mixtures of sensitivity and insensitivity, each modulating the other depending on context. Bion depicts a turning off of sensitivity, a deadening process, the life of the psyche turned into hallucination, something seen as (somewhat) outside. Inside terrors become exteriorized "images" or delusional "whisperings." At the same time, potential impingements are (somewhat) kept from getting in. In this double movement toward evacuation of sensitivity, inside is turned out, and outside kept out.

Since the operation of reversal never stops, sensitivity, disfigured and embalmed in hallucination, remains ever menacing. One can attempt to evacuate oneself, the psyche, and reach a null point. But as Hamlet points out, one cannot quite make nightmares go away. One may wish the psyche out of existence, but one's very wish becomes a haunting ghost. No matter how complete, evacuation is always partial.

Insofar as one succeeds in hallucinating psyche out of existence, (i.e., effectively exteriorizing it), one is in the position of being unable to digest emotional impacts. In effect, one's psychic digestion has been gotten rid of or become damaged and one starves to death emotionally. Since emotional starvation and death are incomplete, one is tantalized and tormented by indigestible feeling, which cannot quite be gotten rid of, or taken in. One labors not to deal with one's sense of annihilating catastrophe, since attempts to work with it have failed.

Bion points out the importance of dreamwork in initiating the processing of affects, that is, emotional digestion. If dreamwork is damaged, emotional processing is damaged. Insofar as dreamwork contributes to processing emotional reality, the hallucinatory exoskeleton that substituted for it can somewhat dissolve. The protective, evasive hallucinatory exoskeleton partly dissolves into dreamwork. One becomes able to have insides, rely more on emotional work.

Rage often indicates a break or failure of emotional digestion and rises as something that ought not or cannot be digested. It signals something is wrong and requires attention. Too often rage works against its signal value by succumbing to its own momentum, so that the work needed does not get done.

It is important to be honest and confess that, to this very instant, we do not know what work needs to be done. And often what "work" we do makes things worse. But as the Talmud suggests, we are obligated to try. My try involves looking, seeing, experiencing, attending. When rage strikes, feel it—that is the message of this book. Feel feelings, feel the raging through and through, pulsing through muscles, bones, glands, every particle of being. Feel the surge and keep on feeling it. Feel it more.

You may want to study it or express it. You may become familiar with other feelings, yearnings, desires, intentions it is entangled with. You may get to be on speaking terms with many levels of pain—physical, emotional agonies of will and soul. You will learn a lot about emotional nuances, velocity, volume, intensity, delicious swirls, eddies, and rocks involved in how it feels to be alive. If you are intellectual, you will want to observe the course of a rageful moment, its waxing and waning, ebbs and flows. If you have an aesthetic bent, you may find rage translating into forms and colors you hadn't quite seen before. Or you may meet it head on, and keep meeting it, a child amidst breakers in the ocean, until you tire and collapse on shore. In time tapestries of possibilities grow around rage nuclei at the center of cities, wars, sculptures, books. To repeat myself, we may not know what to do with rage— caught as we are between dialectics of expression and control— but we can begin to feel it, experience our experience, become more familiar with its contours and contexts.

If we put a tracer on rage through history, we will be amazed at the importance of its role in action and culture. It permeates the literature of love, war, power, vulnerability. It is associated with boundary violation of every sort—personal, national, ideological. It arises in response to threat, often in protest, defense, or affirmation of what we invest with a sense of identity or take to be the essence of ourselves. It may be part of the will to dominance, a reaction against restraint or limits. Often it feeds off the perceived weakness of others, and wards off weakness of one's own. It can be part of a drive to be on top, or a reaction to sudden loss of balance or position (physically, psychically, socially). It begins with the infant's scream, if not before, and remains part of our being all life long.

What I have done in this book is depict rage from many angles, draw it closer into the fabric of experience, modulate it by contact with qualifying capacities, connect it to dense knots of feeling, bring it into the context of our evolving beings. There is no pretense of knowing what to do or what ought to be done. But by focusing and refocusing on rage in shifting contexts, something begins to give, open up. Movement becomes possible in places that seemed inaccessible, where psychic flow and processing stopped or could not go.

**T**his book was written before September 11, 2001. Rage was in the air. Every day, newspapers reported another case of road rage, office rage, ethnic rage, computer rage, erotic rage, economic and political rage, property and territorial rage, holy rage.

In the weeks before 9/11 I found myself thinking a lot about our inflated society. CEO's, celebrities, athletes making multimillions. Egos on parade, like balloons in the Macy's parade on Thanksgiving (why this need to gawk at inflated figures on a day of thanks?). A walk through poor sections of Brooklyn tells a different story. The poor in the United States are better off than the poor in Third World countries, but the gap between those who have a lot and those who have not much is searing. No wonder the sense of living on a volcano stays with us. It is a latent volcano that underlies such gaps throughout the world.

Jesus says the poor will always be with us, which implies that the rich will always be with us too, and the super-rich, and the super-super-rich. The rich and powerful and famous hope that celebrating their success and bathing in their aura and sharing crumbs (ships on rising waters) will somewhat modulate other people's envy and resentment, as if a little "transference fusion" can make up for what one doesn't have.

Freud notes that a certain discontent is part of the price one pays for civilization. One has to rein oneself in, take others into consideration to make a go of it—a practical version of the Ten Commandments. Competition, after all, requires cooperation, and people have to find some way to get along together, even to make war. Freud believed a common unhappiness, a sort of everyday depressive tendency, attached to the necessary reining in of impulses.

Toward the end of his life, he began to glimpse the workings of a destructive undercurrent threatening whatever we build. It would not surprise him to learn that "normal" everyday misery blossomed into widespread rage.

If one tries to trace the roots of anything, one ends with endless, knotty root systems. We cannot point to something and say, "That's the cause of our problems." Nevertheless, we tend to organize our thinking around "causality" and do a lot of pointing. Often "cause" degenerates into blame, a kind of moral "causality," whether "your fault" or "my fault."

In our age, economic factors assume the mantle of primary cause of our problems. By the second decade of the twentieth century, Oswald Spengler declared the economic spirit dominant in our age, while the intuitive spirit declined. Is it economic hypnosis, spiritual economic dominance, that makes us place more weight on material factors than they can deliver?

Does economic inequity create our problems, or are they the outgrowth of the sort of beings we are? What part of the circle shall we enter? Does economic mania and greed act as a barrier against further growth? Is it part of our resistance to coming to terms with ourselves as psychospiritual-material beings, as part of the evolving tissue of reality? The human race has the means to eliminate poverty. What stops it? Economic factors are important and must be addressed. But who will address them? how? with what attitude?

In the Introduction to this book I note that literature since antiquity documents murder in high places. The powerful murder each other. It is not simply a matter of crime among the poor or against the rich or by rich against poor, real as that is. The "haves" jockey for position. There is a surplus, an extravagance in the need to be on top, always subject to being toppled. The tower of Babel is everywhere, in low and high places, like children's blocks. There is no escaping the kind of beings we are. Block builders, block busters.

We possess a lust for power coated with ideology and images.

More than coated, filled with tasty lies, all the more deceptive because lies are often truths. Running through truthful lies and lying truths is the sense of being right. I don't know anything in human history that has done more harm than the sense of being right. I'm right—you're wrong. As if there were a shortage of right and wrong, as if there weren't enough rights and wrongs to go around. Today, as ever: they call us evil, we call them evil. Rage (outrage) is always justified. A sense of justice runs through wounded sensitivity, whether the level of the wound is economic, political, military, religious, ethnic, or personal. Often all of these fuse.

We might envision an earth where every person is, as Buckminster Fuller suggests, a winner—but how? A humane economics will not eliminate the pressures involved in wanting more and learning to share, although it may be an outgrowth of working with such confounding tendencies. Crucial as a humane economics is, we cannot expect it to "solve" who we are and what we do to each other.

As a psychologist, I am wary of economic "solutions" to disturbance. There is no "cure" for human nature. Certainly no economic cure. Sooner or later, we will have to discover how to work with factors in ourselves that add to the sum of human misery. Factors of all kinds, including our strange and wayward psychological makeup. Politics exploits economics as well as being subject to the latter. And spirit, attitude, psychological tendencies exploit and inform them both. It is, finally, something psychological that prevents the sociopolitical growth that could result in a kinder distribution of world goods. Call the x-factor by many names: vanity (individual, class, ethnic, national), fear, greed, envy, resentment, possessiveness, hypercontrol—pick your favorite sin, trace it through the body politic, and you will find no lack of micromacro wars between and within groups and individuals to focus on.

What does psychology offer in the face of the massive problems of human life? Very little, perhaps, but that little is very precious. We are discovering new ways to be with each other. In psychotherapy we focus on moment-to-moment shifts of attitude and feeling, forms of interaction, ways we short-circuit our sense of ourselves and our responsiveness to life. We experiment in letting feeling grow. We cultivate a sensitivity to dream processes and the role dreaming plays when we are asleep and when we are awake. We begin to realize that what takes place in dreaming plays a role in larger processes of emotional digestion. We discover how we dream each other into being.

All too often dreams are nightmares and instead of being dreamt they are enacted by groups and cultures. Instead of psychic life building, psyche is "evacuated" into the world as disaster packets, global traumatic unleashments. Psychic indigestion spews calculated nightmares, injury, shock, mutilation, with one or another good or mad justification. Somehow there is always "justice" attached to what we do to one another—"justice" in injustice.

Often the horrible things we do bring out the best in us. The disasters we inflict on each other are almost excuses for extraordinary goodness and self-transcendence, as if we have to go to extremes of badness to discover the indestructible core—a golden ore that war, misery, fear, and trembling distills. We seem never to tire of speaking of heroes, the self-sacrificing workers who gave of themselves around the clock, after the 9/11 bombings (we can, indeed, call the airplanes steered into buildings bombs). Even the mental health field was unified—all warring schools chipping in without regard to normally contentious ideologies in order to do what they could. It was too good to last, and fighting began to break out within and between even the most heroic groups (police and firefighters) as well as others (I actually heard a Scientology worker exclaim that if it weren't for his group, there would have been no rescue effort at all!). But this was secondary to the work done and the spontaneous sacrifices made.

Such quiet in New York City. Shock knit a city together. Cars did not honk for weeks. It was a relief when someone cut in front of me in a subway line nearly a month later, the usual "me first" resurfacing. Less than two months later, you had to watch out again, cars busting your tail if you dared to go slower than a rocketship.

( *Beyond 9/11* : 173 )

This unity through disaster was real. But not everyone was part of it. Palestinian militants were not the only ones to dance in the streets. There was some dancing in sections of Brooklyn, and on a walk through one of them I saw folding tables on the street with the Koran being handed out and study groups in progress in obvious sympathy with the furious justice meted out to arrogant America. Unity is uneven. There are always diverse pockets within it, a pluralism of antagonistic unities.

Where was I on 9/11 at the moment the first bomb struck? I was driving up FDR Drive in Manhattan on the way to work, listening to WINS radio news. A quirk of feeling kept me from being in front of the World Trade Center. I had an urge to drive my younger son to school, against my wife's wishes. She felt he should take the subway (more autonomy), but I indulged my symbiotic, infantilizing side, wanting to spend a little more time with him (he was glad to get the ride). This left me near the Brooklyn Bridge, which takes me up the east side of Manhattan, rather than on my usual route through the Brooklyn Battery Tunnel up West Street past the WTC on my way uptown. I am thankful I gave in to my feelings.

When I let my son off, I remarked, "What a beautiful day!" Since that time whenever I begin to say, "What a beautiful day!" the words stick in my throat. They have become signifiers of disaster. Someday I will say those words again, but for now they fuse with fear.

I kept the speaking engagements I had on the West Coast two weeks later. Never was I treated so well on airlines and another thing I was not used to—the flights left and arrived on time. On the drive from the airport into San Francisco, my friendly colleague and I were chatting, until I looked at the beautiful skyline and saw—really saw—empty spaces in place of tall buildings. Where there are big buildings, I (many New Yorkers) see planes flying into them. My West Coast colleague did not know what it felt like yet—and I hope he never will—to see this kind of shattered emptiness. Yet I understood what a small thing my fear was compared to the mutilated, burnt, tortured bodies and souls of all the wars of man. I could not help but weep unpredictably during my talks. My audience of professionals felt with me. Pockets of our beings, our country, were thawing out.

One of the things I did when I got home was something I had meant to do for years. I read the Koran. I had a two-track experience. On the one hand, I noted so much space devoted to violence, destruction of evil, unbelievers, infidels. The Koran does not take second place to the Torah when it comes to punishing desecration. Fanatical terrorists would have little difficulty finding ways to justify their beliefs. On the other hand, I experienced a direct pipeline to Allah—a rush, infusion, surrender to the One. This must be the track that Sufi poets I love—Rumi, Hafitz— ride on. A rocketship to God, divine wedding, divine dance. Heart opening, overflowing, mystical abundance, an ever open hand. A never-ending love affair with the All/One, a love affair with goodness, the pain-ecstasy that comes when the lover calls, taps, pries our heart open. This must be the current that gives rise to the best in human life, the current that channels and sublimates the worst.

So many levels and dimensions are compressed and fused in the Koran and Torah. Such violent imagery rotating around rage. So much rage rotating around a sense of violation—around the theme of purity. A rage nucleus in the midst of violation. A Sabbath breaker is stoned to death on orders from Moses in *Numbers*. One can rationalize such stories many ways. For example, it portrays spiritual soul-murder that goes with imperfect faith. But no amount of reinterpretation can make the violence imaged in these tales go away. It is not just a matter of narrative: it is a violence that marks human life, takes many forms, many turns—inner and outer violence we do to ourselves and one another, as if we are inserted into violent force fields that work through us in unending ways.

Another biblical example (there is no lack) is the story of Pinchas, who slays two lovers while they are desecrating the House of Israel. His righteous wrath cleanses the body politic and the body spiritual and, for the moment, sets things right. Later rabbinic writings make things harder for would-be Pinchases, providing barriers against taking the law into one's own hands and civil protection for sinners. But the theme is important in holy writings: a sense of purity preserved by murder. As I discuss above in "God's Personality," the Almighty, our semiprojective model, purifies by destruction. Purifies by rage. Subgroups of the human population discover that God purifies by love too, although external results may not be so immediately apparent. In holy writings rage and love fuse-split.

There seems to be a common thread between the attitude expressed by Pinchas and an eleventh-century heretical Islamic sect associated with murdering enemies as a religious duty. The twists and turns of history subdued but did not eliminate this current, which is swelling now. The idea that groups can solve problems by insulating themselves against external influence is a throwback to the ancient inclination to preserve purity by violence. Fear of influence, fear of contagion—by other groups, practices, body parts or fluids (women's blood), disease, food, garments, on and on —all associated with ethical impurity. Ethnic and ethical purity—a devastating link.

Blacks, Jews, women, gays, abortion clinics, peace addicts, Western attitudes, impiety, Nazis, Communists, Capitalists—all sorts of pollutants. How to keep soul, nation, group pure?! Militant extremists of every breed are frightening, and fanaticism of belief corrodes growth of mutual responsiveness. Fighting impurity with militant purity creates new turns of destruction. The image, the reality of the World Trade Center in the process of destruction (how many times we viewed the eight- or nine-second collapse) prompted someone to call this event the greatest art work of the past fifty years. To level a mammoth signifier of the corporate world—symbol of our economic age—stops one short, gives food for thought, food for imagination. Hallucination and reality are one. One wonders whether our hypereconomic mania will someday go the way of the dinosaurs, whether a black winter isn't already beginning.

No, not yet, not soon. The fight against terrorism is in high gear, although we are no longer sure whether our ability to bomb an enemy into submission is a sign of strength or weakness. We are more unsure than ever, not just about what our actions will unleash in others, but also about how what we do affects ourselves. Public leaders, of course, must always display confidence. But it seemed to me to pass the bounds of decency to urge, the day after the bombing, that our citizenry should go out and buy things—as if spending money were a sign of national defiance, a healing act. At that moment, our economic lewdness seemed ugly indeed. A moment to glimpse, at least, how economic militancy deforms our connection to feelings.

We will defeat this efflorescence of terrorist extremism, but victory will not end the terrorist impulse. What we are witnessing—again—is what human beings do and continue to do, in all places, throughout all ages. We have proved we are good at murder. But as yet we have failed to convince ourselves that murder does not solve the problems human beings face. The gods of our holy books do not provide good examples in this respect—or, at least, their worth as models is suspect, requiring criticism and creative interpretation.

Shakespeare has it right when he points out that we are the problem, not the stars, not the other guy (we are the other guy). We as a group, the human race. Murder is one ancient answer, but so is dialogue. Seeds of dialogue have been planted and slowly spread roots throughout our lives. Every country, every person, is the place where tyranny and responsiveness meet. We cannot wish problems away. We cannot kill them. Our problems appear to be immune to destruction. But dialogue modifies them or, at least, slowly modifies our attitude to them.

Is it merely another utopian wish to imagine an age of economic tyranny giving rise to a dialogical age? A vision of all voices having contributions to make—in contrast to a world given over to competing terrorisms, economic and ethnic terrorisms, terrorisms of affluence and poverty, purity and power. Any moment in any place where one person hears another and grows in ability to take in and respond—there is a faith worth having. Any moment—even in the belly of the dinosaur—where one person hears another is a start.

Therapy turns on moment-to-moment dramas of faith and collapse. Mutual response, injury, recovery—how we recover from what we do to each other and to ourselves. In the book you are reading, rage is the focus, moment-to-moment rage, rage throughout a lifetime. Rage seems nearly ubiquitous in our day. My aim is not to stamp out our rageful capacity, not even to be victorious. Simply to turn it this way and that, pay attention, learn, open up, sit, talk, feel, participate in the evolution of what it is possible to experience, at times reaching beyond the possible. It is enough to clear some space to listen, to sense, to grow in intangible ways that may help awaken a larger thirst for respecting and caring, for tasting what we offer one another. I think there is a broader wish for this kind of hearing than may be apparent in worlds oriented around power and/or purity. Trying to hear with all one's might (the "rage" to hear) is a rage modifier, lust for power/purity a rage accelerant. To seek to hear is a capacity that adds to those who use it, whether giving or receiving. We may be artists at imaginative destruction—but I believe our longing for imaginative hearing, opening, creating is greater.

Do I think what I've written about rage before September 11 is still relevant? More than ever. Not just because it is "emotion recollected in tranquility"—often I've written about rage with passionate rage. But the point is I've written, spoken, not beaten or killed. To be sure, there are forms of murder beyond the literal. Words can poison the soul. Words are no protection against violence. There are clever ways to manipulate a country or a world besides the military, and the slant one puts on maneuverings can make the devil jealous. Let us hope another's words will balance our own and that we draw each other out, take each other to new places. Let us pray for a safe, healthy, productive life for all. But we can be sure that whoever and wherever we are, the same old human problems will rise to greet us, and we will have ourselves to face not just at the end or beginning of the day, but throughout our lives. It is one of the great paradoxes of living that we do change when we focus on what can't change. Sometimes we will hold hands, sometimes travel alone. But we will never stop moving toward a beginning when it comes to what we do with ourselves and each other. My extended meditation on rage hinges on a handful of "dynamisms" that, in one or another form, exert force in daily life. How we meet or learn about them, what we do with them, is an open matter. We have a lot of evolving to do.

# NOTES & REFERENCES

p. 1: Robert Young links Oedipus's patricide with his father's attempted infanticide in "New Ideas about the Oedipus Complex," *Melanie Klein and Object Relations* 12 (1994): 1–20.

p. 1: The term "art" is used here in a generic sense, including secular and sacred literature.

p. 2: Art's critique of murder: Actual murder blots out states that constitute it. Art gives murder awareness that it lacks. In art, life looks at itself, takes itself apart and pieces itself together in ways it cannot do in literal living. One reason art feels more real than life is its nascent ability to extract in concentrated form experiential nuclei that slip away in living.

p. 3: With regard to the Bible's overreliance on destruction to solve problems, see the following sections of this book: "Golden Calf," "Pinchas," "Pinchas Afterwaves," and "God's Personality."

p. 4: In one way or another, religions have tried to deal with rage and violence but perpetuate it in their "solutions." In pointing out rage currents in religion, I do not intend any kind of rage reductionism. All major religions are more than the sum of their parts but less than they hope. I have tried to look God's rage in the eyes and say what I see. You can guess whose face in the mirror shines back—yours and mine. Our rage connects with God's rage. Too often pillow talk with God obscures a lust for murder. That doesn't mean we should end our love affair with God or each other—but it does mean we need to experience where it leads us. To experience does not mean to enact, although enough experiencing may inform, modulate, and modify enactment.

p. 4: Concerning Islam, rage and purity: This book was written before September 11, 2001, the date of the attacks on the World Trade Center and the Pentagon, events that heighten the relevance of many of the themes in this work. For an addendum relating this exploration of rage to the bombing, see the section "Beyond 9/11."

p. 9:   S. Freud (1914), "The *Moses* of Michelangelo," *Standard Edition,* 13:211–36.

p. 18: On self-traumitization and self-nourishment, see M. Eigen (1999), *Toxic Nourishment,* London: Karnac Books.

p. 19: "The earliest problems . . . a link between two personalities": W. R. Bion (1965), *Transformations,* London: Heinemann, p. 66.

p. 21: K. Abraham (1973), *Selected Papers,* London: Hogarth Press, pp. 248–79, 396–98, 402–3, 418–501.

p. 42: Carl Rogers developed what he called "client centered psycho- therapy," which emphasized empathic reflection of the client.

p. 58: W. R. Bion (1994), *Clinical Seminars and Other Works,* London: Karnac Books, p. 169.

p. 59: O. Rank (1968), *Art and Artist,* New York: Agathon Press.

p. 59: J. Lacan (1978), *The Four Fundamental Concepts of Psycho-Analysis,* trans. A. Sheridan, ed. Jacques-Alain Miller, New York: Norton.

p. 59: Bion, *Transformations,* p. 103; see my elaboration of Bion in *The Psychoanalytic Mystic* (1998), London and New York: Free Associa- tion Books, chaps. 3–7.

p. 67: With regard to waves of threats uniting multiplicatively, see my chapter "Primary Process and Shock" in *Psychic Deadness* (1996), Northvale, N.J.: Jason Aronson, where I describe shocks to per- sonality uniting and resonating with each other.

p. 75: "Every soul is a different species": When I wrote this, I thought I was quoting Thomas Aquinas, but such a remark did not show up when I searched his texts. I quickly got in over my head as to what "species" and "soul" meant. Some passages seemed to imply the reverse of what I wrote: different species have different souls. But then angels seemed to be one species with many souls (*Summa Theologica,* part I, question 50, article 4). Aquinas also argues that the soul is the form of the body and created in the body. If "the soul had a species of itself" it would be more like the angels (*Summa Theologica,* part I, question 90, article 4). Soul is a formal principle of the body for animals, including us. We are composite beings, body and soul. Augustine's view that "each soul is unique" seems closer to what I had in mind (B. A. G. Fuller [1945], *A History of Philosophy*, New York: Henry Holt and Company, 1:355).

I floated my quandary on the Internet, and Corbett Williams suggested that my "quotation" was too twentieth- or twenty-first-century to be Aquinas. He said (I quote him with his permission): "This particular type of thinking is distinctly non-Aristotelian — it is not the class or category that matters . . . it is what makes the individual, a soul, unique that is most important, i.e., it is the differences that must be considered sacred." To mitigate rage, encompassing sameness-difference is crucial. The notion that all humans share a common nature may elicit brotherly sympathy. But the fact that we are more alike than otherwise often degenerates into my definition of who we are vs. your definition, and it is not unusual for conflicts about identity to trigger rage. An ideology of sameness is explosive. On the other hand, too great an emphasis on difference can boomerang, making the other seem alien, even an enemy. One rages to break out of sameness, and rages against threatening differences. Some kind of working appreciation of both sameness and difference seems to offer more hope of balance or, at least, tolerance.

p. 92: "Energy is Eternal Delight": William Blake, *The Marriage of Heaven and Hell*.

p. 93: Freud envisioned hidden satisfactions mediated by neurotic symptoms. The pleasure principle plays an important role in the work of neurosis. Fusion of pleasure and frustration is so intense that Freud's writings raise the question of what the nature of satisfaction can be. Lacan asks this question with regard to Freudian drives, which are never fully satisfied yet are implicated in the comingling of pleasure/frustration that is part of the infrastructure of experiencing ("the function of the drive has for me no other purpose than to put in question what is meant by satisfaction" [*The Four Fundamental Concepts of Psycho-Analysis*, p. 166]). For passages on the "secondary gain" of illness or pleasure in symptoms, see S. Freud (1905), "Fragment of an Analysis of a Case of Hysteria," *Standard Edition*, 7:43; (1916–17), "Introductory Lectures on Psycho-Analysis," *Standard Edition*, 16: 381, 384; and (1926), "Inhibitions, Symptoms and Anxiety," *Standard Edition*, 20:chap. 3. Freud also wrote ([1924], "On Narcissism: An Introduction," *Standard Edition,* 14:73–102) of sensory erotic streaming partly organized by a pleasure/narcissistic ego, so that pleasure is not only the underside of skin, but also the underside of the ego (in origins, a body ego). Later ([1920], "Beyond the Pleasure Principle," *Standard Edition,* 18:1–64) he envisioned each psychic act as a mixture of life and death forces, melding pleasure, pain, and nothingness (Eigen, *Psychic Deadness,* chap. 1). He depicted cases in which trauma impacted on the pleasure principle, so that the individual became more involved with self-repair than with satisfaction. Rage and pleasure may play a role in attempts to express and repair injury, often making things worse. Exuberance and injury may become indistinguishable. Bion picks up on this thread and explores not merely damage to the pleasure principle but to the capacity to process emotional life. If emotional life cannot be digested, the individual is in danger of starving or suffocating (W. R. Bion [1992], *Cogitations,* London: Karnac Books, pp. 1–90; M. Eigen [2001], *Damaged Bonds,* London: Karnac Books, chaps. 2–4). One suffocates on rage and pleasure that fail to undergo transformation into nourishment.

p. 93: I wrote about a pain machine in *The Psychoanalytic Mystic,* chap. 7.

p. 95: S. Freud (1920), "Beyond the Pleasure Principle," *Standard Edition,* 18:1–64.

p. 95: For an elaboration of "toxic love," see my *Toxic Nourishment.*

p. 100: S. Freud (1918), "From the History of an Infantile Neurosis," *Standard Edition,* 17:75, 99–100.

p. 101: W. R. Bion (1970), *Attention and Interpretation,* London: Tavistock, pp. 12–13.

p. 109: D. W. Winnicott (1992), *Psychoanalytic Explorations,* ed. C. Winnicott, R. Shepherd, and M. Davis, Cambridge: Harvard University Press, pp. 116–18.

p. 111: For a portrayal of one man's "fight to the death" against the life-spoiling tendency, see the comment son Les in my book *Reshaping the Self* (1995), Madison, Conn: Psychosocial Press.

p. 114: The notion of states has a complex role in Blake's prophecies, and to explore it adequately would require discussion beyond what is needed here. I'm associating states with tendencies, which is my reworking, taking a liberty. Some sense of the Platonic perdurance of states is suggested in Blakean pronouncements such as "The spiritual states of the Soul are all Eternal ("To the Deists," plate 52), "And the Center has Eternal States (*Jerusalem* 3:45), and "So Men pass on but States remain permanent forever" (*Jerusalem* 3:45). One is tempted to compare the eternality of Blakean states with the "constant force" of Freudian drives (Lacan, *The Four Fundamental Concepts of Psycho-Therapy*, p. 164) and Bion's "thoughts without a thinker" (*Attention and Interpretation*, pp. 102–5).

pp. 116–20: Bion, *Cogitations*, p. 81.

p. 118: J. Lacan (1977), *Ecrits: A Selection*, trans. A. Sheridan, New York: Norton.

pp. 118–19: I give detailed portrayals of various forms of reversal/interpermeability of psychic dimensions in *The Psychotic Core* (1986), Northvale, N.J.: Jason Aronson, chap. 8, and *The Electrified Tightrope* (1993), ed. A. Phillips, Northvale, N.J.: Jason Aronson, pp. 243–78.

p. 119: For writings relevant to boundless dread of mental influence, see V. Tausk (1933), "On the Origin of the Influencing Machine in Schizophrenia, *Psychoanalytic Quarterly* 2:519–56; P. Federn (1957), *Ego Psychology and the Psychoses*, London: Maresfield Reprints, chaps. 1 and 2; and Eigen, *The Psychotic Core*, chaps. 4 and 8.

p. 120: I've discussed Winnicott's (*Psychoanalytic Explorations*) writings on what happens when the very sense of aliveness is warped, poisoned, traumatized in my book *Toxic Nourishment*, chaps. 5, 9, and 10.

p. 121: For more on the worm side of our self-image, see Eigen, *Psychic Deadness*, pp. 168–71, and A. Phillips (1999), *Darwin's Worms*, London: Faber & Faber; New York: Basic Books.

p. 121: "Making the Best of a Bad Job," in Bion's *Clinical Seminars and Other Works*, pp. 321–31.

p. 122: "'Deeply' here ... emotional involvement": Bion, *Cogitations*, p. 81.

p. 124: The first part of the story, which tells of Hebrews turning to idolatry under the influence of Moabite women, begins in the last part of the section devoted to Balak's unsuccessful attempt to get the prophet Bilam to curse Israel (*Numbers*, 25:1–9). It is as if the narrator is saying, "Look, God even makes a heathen prophet bless Israel when he is trying to utter a curse, and what does Israel do?:

worship the god (Baal) the poor prophet did!" Israel is being set up for a destructive cleansing by Pinchas.

p. 125: *Mattos* is *Numbers,* 30:2–32.

p. 128: For a discussion of Flannery O'Connor's destroyers, see my book *The Psychoanalytic Mystic,* chap. 6.

p. 128: "Rintrah roars and shakes his fiery head from side to side" is my misquote of Blake. Apparently, as I've recently discovered, I've been reciting this line inside my head incorrectly for nearly five decades. The quotation should be: "Rintrah roars & shakes his fires in the burdened air." (It is the first line from *The Marriage of Heaven and Hell.*)

p. 128: "Energy is Eternal Delight": Blake, *The Marriage of Heaven and Hell.*

p. 128: J. Lacan, *Ecrits,* p. 99. For a discussion of the fusion of desire and law, see my chapters "Originary *Jouissance*" and "Serving *Jouissance*" in *The Psychoanalytic Mystic.*

p. 129: The soul's progression is described in Plato's *Symposium.*

p. 130: Sometimes I'm tempted to write God's name, the Tetragramaton, as "Yoyvay," which incorporates Ashkenazie prayer sounds I heard as a child. Moreover, a mischievous me can't help finding the famous "oy vey" in the Unsayable One's Ineffable Name. (G-d forgive me for this irreverent streak which, thank G-d, is part of our freedom and life drive!) The usual "Jahveh" or "Jehovah" just won't do it—but they have their value too. What am I doing? Blessing God for giving me the ability to be irreverent, which is sometimes part of the way we love.

p. 130: Why Esau is associated with evil and Jacob with God's blessing bewilders many readers. After all, Jacob was sneaky and stole from Esau, not the reverse. Esau behaved pretty decently in the story. To add insult to injury, mystical tradition associates Esau with Edom and Rome, which is the dominant spirit today. An unpublished book by Neal Aponte, *In the Shadows of Genesis,* makes the case that Esau has been sorely wronged. I've discussed the ins and outs of Jacob and Esau's relationship and why I think Jacob is the carrier of the blessing elsewhere (*The Psychoanalytic Mystic,* pp. 47–51). I argued for Jacob's greater psychic invagination and possibilities of development. Aspects of this twinship combined in the Zionist movement, which could not have succeeded without Jacob's adroitness and Esau's strength. There are many paradoxes in this twinship that go beyond the point of the discussion here. For me the bottom line is that Jacob had a more intense heart-heart connection with Jahveh, for better and worse. The God-link heated desire for more God-life, which brought character flaws to the surface. Esau was perhaps more naively good natured, a lively hunter, a man's man, associated with naive egoism, naive realism. Optimally, one tries to make use of what each tendency offers.

p. 131: Korach's story is in *Numbers,* 16–18.

p. 133: See the chapter "Disaster Anxiety" in my *Psychic Deadness* for dreads like the ground opening beneath one.

p. 134: The story of the spies appears in *Numbers,* 13.

p. 144: The red heifer story usually is given as an example of a "reasonless" dictate springing from the fathomless Desire of the Supreme Lover. What Lover wants, lover does. One doesn't ask why in matters of desire. The red heifer appears in *Numbers,* 6:19.

p. 146: S. Freud (1907), "Obsessive Actions and Religious Practices," *Standard Edition,* 9:117–27; (1927) "The Future of an Illusion," *Standard Edition,* 21:43–44.

p. 146: "O my God, the soul you have given me is pure": This is from the Jewish morning prayer service and is in most Orthodox and Conservative *siddurim* (the *siddur* is the standard book of prayers). I somewhat retranslated this line from *The Metsudah Siddur* (1983), trans. Rabbi Avrohom Davis, New York: Metsudah Publications, p. 17.

p. 147: "Pleasure in the goal region" is a term that was used in experiments in which rats had to get through a maze or do tasks for which they were rewarded with food or sex when they reached the goal region. There was one setup in which a rat pressed an electrode implanted in the pleasure center of its brain and found the experience so compelling that it kept pressing and starved to death. When I heard this term in graduate school in the 1960s, it immediately became part of my working imagery: pleasure in the goal region, associated with heavenly experience, no more getting there—one *is* there. This amalgamated in my mind with the Zen realization of being present here and now, which further melded with the just-so-ness of things and *sunyata,* emptiness, of Buddhism (condensing just-so and nothingness). Such terms represent a shift from an attitude of striving to get somewhere to the sense that one *is* somewhere now. Nevertheless, *more* does not vanish. Wherever one is, there is more and more (as Beatrice and Dante discover in heaven, as heaven becomes ever more heavenly).

p. 147: E. Levinas (1969), *Totality and Infinity,* trans. A. Lingis, Pittsburgh: Duquesne University Press, pp. 187–219. See also my chapter "The Significance of Face" in *The Electrified Tightrope.*

p. 151: I've written elsewhere on vaginal heart opening, which I was led to through intensity of psychic pain. Losing myself in painful emotion centering in my chest led unexpectedly to a sense of my heart opening to radiant light (*The Psychoanalytic Mystic,* pp. 41, 181). It felt like passing through the end of a vaginal channel or womb opening to universes of light. We experience many interweavings of mysterious emotional currents — rage, pain, light currents three of them.

p. 152: Winnicott depicts the "last scream just before hope was abandoned" in *Psychoanalytic Explorations,* pp. 115–18.

p. 153: "an intense catastrophic emotional explosion O": Bion, *Attention and Interpretation,* pp. 12–15. For discussion of a diversity of meanings of explosive processes in Bion's work, see my book *The Electrified Tightrope,* chap. 17. For more on Bion's use of the big bang image, see my *Psychoanalytic Mystic,* chap. 3, *and Toxic Nourishment,* pp. 148–49.

p. 154: See my *Damaged Bonds* for explorations of damaged dreamwork and impaired processing of emotional impacts.

p. 158: Wanting his mother to himself, wanting his mother to divorce his father, his father actually leaving, my patient becoming the actual or fantasy man of the family — it sounds very Freudian. It also suggests the mythic cult of the Mother Goddess, whom men serve. It is a tale of grave damage, with addiction to the Idea of the Mother, a fantasy mother who would be more giving and respectful and who would repair the damage inflicted by traumatizing parents, traumatizing world. The wish to be mother's only god signifies damage no mother can repair.

p. 165: S. Freud, *Standard Edition* 4:228, 543, 565–67, 598; 5:548; 14:231; 18:32; 19:232ff., 267. See my discussion of Freud and hallucination in *The Psychotic Core,* chap. 2.

p. 166: On hallucination, dreamwork, and psychic damage, see Bion, *Cogitations,* pp. 30–150, and my *Damaged Bonds,* chaps. 1–4.

p. 167: On emotions too devastating for sensitivity, see my chapter "The Sensitive Self" in *Coming Through the Whirlwind* (1992), Wilmette, Ill.: Chiron Publications, pp. 178–242. See also *The Psychotic Core,* chaps. 4 and 8.

p. 168: Attention has associative overtones ranging from standing fast for inspection to attending to needs of place or being or details of living, as well as activities of perception and mental observation. To pay attention has become somewhat "psychologized" in every-day life, pertaining to self's need for attention. Rapt attention, too, suggests links with beauty, rapture, deep absorption, high significance—a mixture of caring and carefulness, a respectful, deeply felt awareness.

p. 170: "Transference fusion" is my idiosyncratic term referring to Freud's writings on the way we identify with parents, teachers, leaders, and group values (whether vocational, political, religious, or erotic). It is not just a matter of transferring dependent attachments from parents to power figures throughout a lifetime, although that is part of it. There is a tendency to lift oneself up, organize oneself through varying "identities" that grant some personal cohesiveness by fusing with images of those who stimulate or carry our ideals. S. Freud (1921), "Group Psychology and the Analysis of the Ego," *Standard Edition,* 14:217–35.

p. 170: S. Freud (1930), "Civilization and Its Discontents," *Standard Edition,* 21:59–145; (1920) "Beyond the Pleasure Principle," *Standard Edition,* 18:1–64; (1937), "Analysis Terminable and Interminable," *Standard Edition,* 23: 216–53. See also Eigen, *Psychic Deadness,* chap. 1.

p. 171: The fact that the United States exploits countries economically and even manipulates them politically and militarily does not mean it created the conditions of which it takes advantage. Poverty preceded the existence of the United States, and social systems perpetuating high-low gaps have a long history. That one group or individual is partly wrong does not make another entirely right. An ethics of shared responsibility will have to penetrate every living soul if the notion "justice for all" is to carry maximum weight. Impossible? Possibly. But not meaningless. It is an ethics that goes against the grain of our possessive, power-driven nature, where, too often, might makes right. Yet it is an ethics that fascinates us, transforms us, and stimulates a kind of reaching that grows out of our sociality, our caring.

p. 171: O. Spengler (1939), *The Decline of the West,* trans. Charles Francis Atkinson, New York: Alfred A. Knopf (originally published in German in 1918).

p. 172: For an example of finger-pointing as a way of solving problems, see "Winning Lies" in my *Psychic Deadness,* pp. 201–11. A cartoon that appeared on <Onion.com> showed God saying something like, "They just don't get it: I mean don't kill." Needless to say, the God of religions has not set the best example. But his abuse of power further highlights problems we face. If even the good God has his problems with rage, what are we mortals up against?

p. 172: This idea of Buckminster Fuller's appears at the beginning of John Cage's *Anarchy* (2001), Middletown, Conn.: Wesleyan University Press.

p. 173: For portrayals of how dreaming can go wrong (i.e., how damaged dreamwork fails to digest emotional experience), see *Damaged Bonds,* chaps. 2–4, and Bion, *Cogitations,* pp. 37–98.

p. 173: We are extremely sensitive and insensitive beings, and what to do with this mix is puzzling. Each of us experiments on his or her cutting edge, learning to work with capacities that are cognized as polar but are, in fact, deeply interconnected. What may work in one context wreaks havoc in another. I devoted half a book to showing how the profession of teaching can throw personality out of shape, as well as be fulfilling (see the sections on Lynn in *Reshaping the Self*). This same effect can be produced by nearly every institutional structure. A good New York politician, questioned on how he felt after losing an election, responded, "I cut off my nerve endings as a young man.... Otherwise you can't do this line of work" (*New York Times,* November 7, 2001). Widespread nerve-cutting must have widespread repercussions.

p. 173: I originally made a typo, substituting "mobs" for "bombs." I can't help wondering if this was a good error, a good link. A promise made to the bombers was that they would feel better, their personal disturbances would melt in divinity, that holy murder was a heavenly path (from a four-page document the September 11 bombers used, given to the *New York Times* by the FBI and published September 29, 2001). The idea of murder as a way of ending disturbance is very old, with many variants (see "A Bug-free Universe" in my *Toxic Nourishment,* pp. 57–84).

p. 175: For the stoning, see *Numbers,* 15:32.

p. 175: The story of Pinchas is related in *Numbers,* 25:1-30. See also "Pinchas," "Pinchas Afterwaves," and "God's Personality" in this book.

p. 175: Beyond their religious value, the Torah and Koran (and other holy writings) provide multiple universes of discourse fused, melded, superimposed in a proliferation of ways, out of which one can distill currents of rage, love, control, punishment, guilt-shame, openness, wisdom, tragedy, inquiry—streams of emotions and attitudes in fossil and living forms. Many well-meaning people tell me that the scriptures related to Jesus are different, indicating that there is a God of love and mercy. But so much wrath finds fertile soil through "belief" in this God: If you're not for me, you're against me—all hell to pay. I am not saying there should not be rage in holy writings. I am noting that there *is* rage—and that its far-flung presence says something about us and our universe that begs for careful attention. In a related context, for fusions of ecstasy and destructiveness, see *Ecstasy,* pp. 3, 6, 10, 63–64, 72–74.

p. 176: The Nizara Ism'ilites, an Islamic sect with a religious commitment to kill the unfaithful, which flourished in the eleventh to thirteenth centuries but was suppressed by the Monguls, is said to have descendents in present-day Syria, Iran, Central Asia, India, and Pakistan. James S. Grotstein found this information by looking up "Assassins" in the *Encyclopedia Britannica.* He wonders if Osama bin Laden is "following in the footsteps" of this earlier tradition (<bioncollective@yahoo.com>, September 17, 2001; permission by Dr. James S. Grotstein and Dr. John Stone, the bioncollective webmaster).

p. 176: On the destruction of the WTC as art: An article I read in the *New York Times* (September or October 2001) quoted a German artist who made such a remark, but I did not save the reference. He was not the only one who felt that way.

p. 177 : See my chapter "Winning Lies" in *Psychic Deadness* for a portrayal of the ax-like confidence with which some senators spoke at the confirmation hearings for Supreme Court nominee Clarence Thomas, where strong displays of position seemed more important than a search for truth.

pp. 177–78: Isaiah's vision of beating swords into plowshares (2:4) or wolf and lamb living together (11:6)—so utopian. Yet it is a guiding principle in the human heart, competing with other principles. Subsets of humans work hard to realize the spirit of this ethics. In some sense, this ideal vision could turn out to be the most realistic path of all.

p. 178: I'm not against the idea or experience of "purity." A Jewish prayer exclaims in awe and heart-burst and loving appreciation, "O my God, the soul you have given me is pure" (see note for p. 146, above). Such an outcry is an inspiring affirmation of basic goodness. However, I am against using any form or notion of "purity" to kill people or maim souls. Different forms of rage and purity fuse.

*About the author:* Michael Eigen is a psychologist and psychoanalyst. He is Associate Clinical Professor of Psychology in the Postdoctoral Program in Psychotherapy and Psychoanalysis at New York University. His numerous books include *Ecstasy* (2001), *Damaged Bonds* (2001), *Toxic Nourishment* (1999), *The Psychoanalytic Mystic* (1998), *Psychic Deadness* (1996), and *The Psychotic Core* (1986). Eigen is also a Senior Member at the National Psychological Association for Psychoanalysis.

Library of Congress Cataloging-in-Publication Data

Eigen, Michael.

Rage/Michael Eigen.

p. cm. — (Disseminations)

Includes bibliographical references.

ISBN 0-8195-6585-7 (cloth : alk. paper) —

ISBN 0-8195-6586-5 (pbk. : alk. paper)

1. Anger—Case studies.  2. Hostility (Psychology)—Case studies.

3. Psychotherapy—Case studies. I. Title.  II. Series.

RC569.5.A53 E38 2002

616.85'82—dc21          2002072595